THE PLACE-NAMES
OF
LANCASHIRE

David Mills

B. T. BATSFORD LTD.
London

© David Mills 1976
First published 1976
First published in paperback 1986

ISBN 0 7134 5236 6

Printed in Great Britain by
Billing & Sons Ltd, Worcester
for the publishers B T Batsford Ltd,
4 Fitzhardinge Street, London W1H 0AH

CONTENTS

PREFACE

As someone with a professional interest in English language and early English literature, and with an amateur interest in Lancashire history, I am very much aware, not only of the fascination of place-names, but also of the dangers which await the non-specialist like myself who ventures into this area of study. At the same time, in the several courses on place-names which I have undertaken during the past ten years for the Institute of Extension Studies at Liverpool University, I have met many people who share my interest in Lancashire place-names but feel overwhelmed by the industry and expertise of many specialist place-name publications. I hope that this book will meet the needs of such people and, without detracting from the work of the specialist, will help them to feel that there is a contribution which a layman can make towards place-name studies.

A book of this kind necessarily relies heavily upon earlier, more original and more scholarly studies. Of those mentioned in the 'Suggestions for Further Reading', particular tribute must be paid to Eilert Ekwall's *The Place-Names of Lancashire,* still the standard work on the subject over 50 years after it was first published; without it, this work could not have been written. Of the many other writers whose work has contributed to this book, F.T. Wainwright deserves special mention here. His studies of 'The Anglian Settlement of Lancashire' (*HSLC* 93, 1941), 'The Field-Names of Amounderness Hundred' (*HSLC* 97, 1945), 'The Scandinavians in Lancashire' (*LCAS* 58, 1945-6) and 'Ingimund's Invasion' (*English Historical Review* 63, 1948) are essential reading for anyone interested in Lancashire place-names and Lancashire history.

I have been fortunate to have access to a number of unpublished undergraduate and graduate theses of the University of Liverpool which provide new material and suggestions. These are: Joan Francis Kelly, *Scandinavian Elements in North-West Place-Names* (1961); Anthony Lenney, *Studies in the Place Names of Blackburn Hundred in the County of Lancashire* (1960) and *Studies in the Minor Place-Names of South*

7

PREFACE

West Lancashire (1962); Elaine Mary Smith, *A Study in the Place-Names of Lonsdale South of the Sands* (1963); and Joan Wise, *The Place-Names of The Fylde in Lancashire* (1961). I have also consulted Frank Oldfield's geographical study, *The Mosses and Marshes of North Lancashire* (1956).

Space will not permit me to acknowledge all the writers whose books, articles and guide-books have contributed to this book, still less the many students of the Liverpool University Institute of Extension Studies who have provided me with information as well as with the interest and stimulus to undertake this work. I am indebted to all of them. I am particularly grateful to Mr. Michael Stephenson and Mr. Roger Hearn of B.T. Batsford Ltd. for their help and advice in preparing this book for publication.

It is a strange coincidence that I, an amateur in place-names matters, should have the same name as an outstanding place-name scholar, A.D. Mills of the University of London. I hope that my namesake will not be unduly embarrassed by any confusion resulting from the publication of this book.

The book is dedicated to the memory of two Lancastrians – my mother, who died on 8 March, 1972, and my father, who died on 21 November, 1983. To them, and to my wife, who has helped me immeasurably in collating index-cards and preparing the final typescript, I should like to express my thanks for their encouragement and understanding over the years.

David Mills
University of Liverpool

GLOSSARY

The following are the commonest abbreviations used in the directory and in section 5 of the introduction:

Brit.	British
Celt.	Celtic
c	circa (before dates); century (in forms such as 13th c.)
DB	Doomsday Book, 1086
dial.	dialect
EPNE	A.H. Smith's *English Place-Name Elements*
ME	Middle English, the form of English spoken between the 11th. and 15th. centuries
NCy	North country
O	old (before words or contractions referring to other languages)
ODan.	Old Danish
OE	Old English, the form of English spoken between the fifth and eleventh centuries
OF	Old French
OIr	Old Irish
ON	Old Norse
ONorw.	Old Norwegian
OS	Ordnance Survey map
OSwed.	Old Swedish
pl.	plural
PNLa	Eilert Ekwall's *The Place-Names of Lancashire*
R	river
Scand.	Scandinavian, divided as OEScand., 'Old East Scandinavian', and OWScand., 'Old West Scandinavian'
VCH	The Victoria County History of Lancashire
We	Westmorland
Yks	Yorkshire

INTRODUCTION

1 The Plan of the Book

This book attempts to make available, in a form which can be readily understood by the interested layman, some of the results of specialist research into the origins and meanings of the modern place-names of Lancashire. It is in two parts. The larger part is a directory of the place-names, arranged alphabetically; the shorter part takes the form of an introduction which is designed to explain and give added significance to the names in the directory by providing general background information about history, topography and language. The purpose of this opening section, however, is to explain the principles on which the material in the directory has been selected and arranged.

The decision to use the old county-divisions as the basis for this series of volumes is entirely one of convenience. The boundaries of Lancashire were drawn comparatively late and the area within them can be sub-divided into smaller units, both administratively and topographically, any of which could provide the basis of a place-name study. Moreover, the economy and population-balance of the county underwent considerable changes as a result of the Industrial Revolution, resulting in new settlements and new social allegiances. Some of this diversity has recently been reflected in the administrative boundaries established within the county-area from April, 1974. Nevertheless, many people still feel an allegiance to the old county of Lancashire which they do not feel to older or to more recently established units. And, in retaining the county-divisions as basis, this series will continue the pattern established by standard reference works such as the Victoria County History series and the volumes of the English Place-Name Society, thereby facilitating cross-reference.

The decision to limit the directory to modern place-names is likewise one of convenience, and one which requires further qualification. By 'modern name' is meant 'a name which appears on the former one-inch Ordnance Survey maps'. There are three general exceptions to this definition. Hall and farm names are omitted unless there is a large area of parkland attached to the hall or it is of particular public interest. Modern names which are self-explanatory, such as Lane Ends near Burnley, are omitted. Finally, many names for which there is no form recorded before the nineteenth-century, such as Crawford, are omitted. Occasionally, a lost name, such as Martin Mere, has been included because it is of particular historical interest, but such names are clearly specified as lost names in the Directory. The result is a shorter directory than that provided by Eilert Ekwall's *Place-Names of Lancashire,* the standard specialist work on the subject, but one which includes a number of modern names, such as Southport and Earlestown, which were either omitted or briefly dismissed as 'modern' by Ekwall because they have no long linguistic history and belong rather to the later economic and social development of the county.

All place-names begin as ordinary words in everyday use, which, over a long period, become modified in meaning, and often also in form, so that they designate one spot on the map as opposed to all others. This development usually occurred before the Norman Conquest, and certainly long before the name was first written down. When it was first written down, however, the name was probably recorded in a semi-phonetic way, and would perhaps still preserve traces of its original spoken form which may have disappeared in the later development of the name. The task of the place-name scholar is therefore to collect as many examples of early forms as possible, and then to use them as the basis for reconstructing the original spoken form of the name.

In presenting examples of early forms of place-names, this directory differs from more specialist works in a number of ways. First, it relies for its evidence upon the forms collected by previous scholars or upon transcriptions of documents made by previous scholars, and not upon original manuscripts. Many of the forms are taken from Ekwall's study of 1922, although it is interesting to note that Ekwall himself relied to a large extent upon published transcripts rather than upon the original documents. However, it has been possible in a number of cases to provide new examples and earlier forms than Ekwall. These come mainly from two sources — transcriptions of manuscripts which were published after Ekwall's volume; and specialist studies of particular aspects of Lancashire place-names, among which a number of unpublished theses of the University of Liverpool demand particular note (see Preface, p. 7). Second, only a small selection of the forms has been given. The earliest recorded form is listed first, and other forms have been chosen to illustrate the development of the modern name-form rather than to give an impression of the variety of the representations recorded.

The forms are given in chronological sequence of record; where the record cannot be precisely dated, an approximate date is given. It must be remembered, however, that for much of the period of a name's development, a number of different spoken forms of the name will co-exist and it may be accidental that one form was written down earlier than another, or even that the document in which it was written has survived. The reader should not assume that one form has suddenly replaced another at a given date.

The process of reconstructing the original spoken form of the name from the evidence of later recorded forms may be difficult for the layman to understand because it involves considerable knowledge of the early forms of English and of other languages, and also of the ways in which language can change and develop. The first difficulty lies in the fact that the form of the English language spoken before the Norman Conquest, which is known by linguists as Old English, differed markedly from that of modern English in indicating the relationship between words by changing the inflections, or endings of words. In modern English, the '−s' ending indicative of both possession and plural represents the major survivor of this system in nouns. In Old English, however, every place-name − and each word that made up the name if the basis was originally a phrase − would have been inflected, with different inflections according to the grammatical function and also to the declension of the noun or adjective. In Old English records, moreover, place-names are not infrequently treated as phrases introduced by the prepositon *ǣt*, 'at'. Since these inflections and the preposition usually disappear by modern English, no attempt has been made to re-create the original inflected form and the inflection is listed only where some trace of it survives in the modern form, as, for example, with the '−am' ending of Lytham which is a survival from the dative inflection '−um'.

A further difficulty arises from the fact that Lancashire place-names reflect the various languages of the people who have settled here. Old English (OE) was the language of the Anglo-Saxons, whose settlement of Britain began in the fifth century AD, but there are names which show the influence of Celtic, the language of the people who inhabited these islands long before the Anglo-Saxon settlement. The language which they spoke was the ancestor of modern Welsh, but its forms have to be reconstructed and most place-name specialists rely upon the expert advice of Celtic scholars. Later, in the ninth and tenth centuries, further settlement occurred, by speakers of Old Norse (ON), ancestor of modern Norwegian and Danish. At this time Old English and Old Norse had much more in common than their modern descendants, differing only in certain sounds or sound-combinations; but although ON was an inflected language like OE, its inflectional endings were different. ON contributes some new inflections and words, but also many other words only slightly different in form from their OE counterparts. The inflections are listed in the directory on the same principle as the listings for the OE inflections. Finally, after the Norman Conquest, some French influence is exerted, though mainly through spelling forms which may influence later pronunciation. These various influences can be used to build up a picture of the settlement-patterns of the county (see section 4 below).

A third difficulty is caused by the early forms of words cited in the etymologies of the names. Again for convenience, the forms listed are those given by A.H. Smith in his standard reference-work, *English Place-Name Elements;* the OE words in Lancashire place-names are those of the Anglian dialect (i.e. the speech of the kingdoms of Mercia and Northumbria). Although some of these early forms look forbiddingly different from those in modern English, a number of the differences result only from differences in spelling-conventions. The main spelling differences are:

(1) *æ*   *æ* and *a* represent different varieties of the 'a'-sound;

(2) ð and þ   These letters represent the same sounds as modern *th* which has replaced them — e.g. the initial sounds of 'thin' and 'then';

(3) ǫ   This letter represents a particular variety of the 'o' -sound and is found only in ON words;

(4) ⁻ and ´   These signs, which are placed above a vowel, indicate that the vowel is long. ⁻ is used in OE words and ´ in ON words. It is important to distinguish vowel-length because the long vowels in English have a different development from the short vowels. Spelling-conventions today may prevent us from clearly recognising vowel-length — the short vowel in *hid*, for example, has its long equivalent in *heed*, not in the 'ai'-diphthong of *hide*;

(5) *   This sign, placed before a word, indicates that the word is not recorded in manuscripts but has been reconstructed by modern scholars on the evidence of later forms and of forms in cognate languages. It will be found most frequently before words of Celtic origin and before the forms of some words only recorded after the Norman Conquest but probably in existence in OE.

It is impossible in this short introduction to anticipate and explain all the difficulties which a reader may have in understanding the early forms of words; a layman interested in the subject will find D.G. Scragg's *History of English Spelling* a helpful introduction. However, it may be noted that, while modern English has *c, k* and *ck,* OE has only *c* and ON only *k;* and that OE uses *f, c* and *sc* often where modern English would use *v, ch* and *sh.* While modern English *y* is used as the equivalent to *i,* as in *tiny,* and for the initial sound in *you,* OE *y* represents a form of the 'u'-sound, similar to that in modern French· *tu.* Finally, in early forms, as a general rule, every letter represents a sound; there are no 'silent letters', such as the *gh* in modern English *night.*

The process by which an etymology is determined may well seem obscure to a layman, who lacks the necessary knowledge of early forms of language and of the processes of linguistic change, and his confidence in the result may be shaken by the discovery that no etymology can be established for some names while for others a variety of possibilities has been suggested. A scholar may be uncertain about the etymology of a name for a variety of reasons. The commonest is that the earliest recorded forms may represent a stage in the name's development which is too late to allow certain reconstruction of the original form — a common problem in Lancashire place-names, partly because the county-area was not populous, prosperous or important during the Anglo-Saxon period and the centuries following the Norman Conquest, when records of names would be most valuable. A further reason, applying particularly to Lancashire, results from the economic and social transformation of the county, particularly its southern portion, in the period of the Industrial Revolution; many modern major names were minor names before the Industrial Revolution and, since it is usually the names of the most important places that are recorded first and most frequently, we lack early records of the names of these late developments. For these reasons particularly, then, etymologies of Lancashire place-names frequently have to be established from late or inadequate evidence. It is therefore often possible to suggest alternative etymologies for the names, all of which are equally probable in the present state of our knowledge. As scholars and laymen continue to discover new evidence, it will become possible to suggest more certain etymologies for such names.

Place-name study is constantly evolving and there have been considerable advances in our understanding of English place-names since Ekwall's thorough and scholarly study of Lancashire place-names in 1922. Ekwall himself continued to consider Lancashire names and revised a number of his earlier views in two later important reference works — *English River Names* (1928) and *The Concise Oxford Dictionary of English Place-Names,* of which the fourth edition, of 1960, has been used in preparing the present book. *English Place-Name Elements,* mentioned earlier, has enabled us to establish more precise meanings for some names than Ekwall was able to do, and its author, A.H. Smith, has also advanced further suggestions for the etymologies of some Lancashire names in the course of the work. A number of linguists and historians have produced work which contributes towards our understanding of Lancashire names; the reader will find references to some of this work in the *Preface* and in the *Suggestions for Further Reading* in this book. It is intended that the directory here will not be just a simplification of Ekwall's pioneer work but also a convenient way of bringing together some of the results of this later scholarship which the layman, who may well have Ekwall's book on his shelves, may not know.

The etymology and meaning given first in each entry represent the present author's own preference. In a number of cases, derivation could be from either an OE word or the corresponding ON word, as with OE *clif* and ON *klif*; in such cases, it is assumed for convenience that in a compound-name, both elements will derive from the same language unless the contrary is clear, and therefore in a name such as *Clifton* it is assumed that since the second element is OE *tūn*, the first element is OE *clif.* It is difficult to distinguish some personal names, such as OE *Hwīta*, from words in general use, such as OE *hwīt*, 'white'; but, while there is little doubt that many places were identified by the names of people who owned them, there is an obvious temptation to assign many unexplained forms to the category of personal names. In the directory, therefore, preference has often been given to etymologies involving words rather than personal names. Some elements have a wide range of meanings and, to avoid repeated debates throughout the directory, a short list of such elements is given at the end of the introduction (see section 5).

Since a place was named to distinguish it from all others in the neighbourhood, the name tells the hearer what was once distinctive about the site. Where the name refers to a physical feature, the site is described; where two places may have been named in distinction to each other, as with *Leigh* and *Westleigh,* cross-reference is made. The directory entries therefore contain more non-linguistic information than might be expected in a more specialist work. Local history, folklore, traditions and popular misunderstandings of the name have all contributed to the development of Lancashire names and find a place in the directory entries.

No place-name volume can claim to be absolute and definitive; each is at best a guide to the present state of our knowledge on the subject. The layman may well feel overwhelmed by the mass of material available and by the linguistic expertise needed to interpret it, but it would be unfortunate if he felt that he could make no contribution to place-name studies. For Lancashire especially, much original research remains to be done. By locating manuscript material and publicising its existence, by collecting examples of names, by using his local knowledge of the area in which he lives, the interested layman is making the expert's task easier and bringing closer the day when a full survey of the place-names of Lancashire will again be undertaken.

Thus, this book should be treated as a report rather than as a reference-work. While the information which it contains may be interesting, it is hoped that its admitted inadequacies may stimulate schools, local organisations and individuals to look more closely at the names of their own area. Its true success will be tested, not by its popularity, but by the speed with which further studies make the material presented here out of date.

2 Administration

The survey of land-ownership commissioned by King William I, the Doomsday Survey, provides a convenient starting-point for the study of both Lancashire place-names and Lancashire administration. Before its appearance in 1086 we have very few records which contain Lancashire names and very few references from which to build up a picture of settlement and administration in the area during the Anglo-Saxon period. It is, however, possible to form some picture of the county at that time from the evidence of place-names, and that is reviewed in section 4 below. It is sufficient here to note that in the period after the Anglo-Saxon settlement, the area of the modern county was divided between the northern kingdom of Northumbria and the midland kingdom of Mercia, and that the evidence of the Doomsday Survey reflects many aspects of settlement and administration as they existed at the end of the Anglo-Saxon period.

However, it should be noted in passing that the evidence provided by the Doomsday Survey for the Lancashire area is not only uneven but, at best, scanty. Areas south of the Ribble are presented with rather more detail than those north of the Ribble. Perhaps this reflects a greater population in the southern regions, or indicates that they were more accessible than the northern, and often more rugged, regions. Perhaps it suggests that some areas of Lancashire, like so much of Yorkshire, had not been spared in the devastation wrought by William on the unruly North in 1069. Whatever the reason, the Survey provides less evidence for Lancashire place-names than we might reasonably have expected, a fact which further contributes to the problems of determining Lancashire etymologies.

The County   Although the word 'county' is a French word, meaning originally 'the domain of a count', which does not enter English until after the Norman Conquest, most modern English counties were Anglo-Saxon in origin. An Anglo-Saxon county was called a *scīr*, a large administrative district made up of a number of smaller administrative areas and under the supervision of an official who was originally called an alderman and later a sheriff. But the county of Lancashire did not

17

exist when the Doomsday Survey was carried out, and the land in the present county was surveyed in two sections. The southern section, 'inter Ripam et Mersham', 'between the Ribble and the Mersey', was surveyed under Cheshire, and the section further north was surveyed under Yorkshire.

The nucleus of the modern county of Lancashire was formed by the lands given by William the Conqueror to Roger of Poitou some time after 1072, a territory further extended by William II some time before 1094. These grants gave Roger all the land between the rivers Ribble and Mersey, together with Lonsdale, Cartmel and Furness. Roger decided to build his castle at Lancaster, which thus became the administrative centre of the lands which he held. The lands held by a lord were collectively known as his 'honour'; hence this area was known as the Honour of Roger of Poitou or the Honour of Lancaster, a title which it continued to have when it was confiscated by the Crown in 1102 following Roger's support of the unsuccessful rebellion by his brother, Robert of Bellême, against Henry I.

Although modern Lancashire was effectively established by these events, it was not termed 'the county of Lancashire' until 1168, under Henry II. A further development occurred in 1351, when Henry, Earl of Lancaster, was made a Duke and was also granted palatine powers – the royal powers, or technically, the powers belonging to the 'palace', from Latin *palatium*. Although these powers lapsed with Henry's death, they were restored to the most famous Duke of Lancaster, John of Gaunt, and made hereditary. Thus the county of Lancashire became the major part of the Duchy of Lancaster, and the county became a county palatine. From 1351 administrative responsibility was vested in the Chancellor of the Duchy of Lancaster.

With the exception of Durham and Montgomeryshire, Lancashire can claim to be the youngest of the English counties. It was formed out of lands in other administrative units and its boundaries – particularly those resulting from the division of Lonsdale by William II – often ignored existing parish-boundaries and physical features of the landscape.

The Hundreds Within the Anglo-Saxon *scīr* was a group of smaller administrative units. These were usually called 'hundreds', probably because they originally consisted of a hundred hides of land, although both the size of the hide and the area of the hundred vary considerably from place to place. Another name for these divisions is 'wapentakes', from ON *vápnatak* which is used for similar divisions in areas occupied by the Scandinavians; the word literally means 'weapon-taking' and the administrative link is not clear, although it has been suggested that it refers to the raising of weapons in acclamation. Yet another name for the divisions is OE *scīr*. Although it is usual to follow the Doomsday practice

18

of referring to the Lancashire units as hundreds, it has been pointed out that both the other terms are found, as in Blakeb(ur)neschire c1288 and in Wappentachias de Blakeb(ur)ne et Leylond 1371. All these words clearly had the same meaning — the use of 'wapentake' may in some cases have been influenced by the use of the same term in Danelaw Yorkshire.

The Doomsday survey records six hundreds south of the R. Ribble, each named after the royal manor within its area. Four of these survived — Derbei (West Derby), Lailand (Leyland), Blacheburn (Blackburn) and Salford; the other two — Walintune (Warrington) and Neweton (Newton-le-Willows) — were later incorporated into West Derby hundred. The land north of the R. Ribble was entered under two heads. The first was the hundred of Agemundrenesse (Amounderness) whose head manor was at Preston. The second was 'the king's land in Eurvicscire' (Yorkshire), the area including Lonsdale, Kendal, Cartmel and Furness. This area was later divided by the grants of land to Roger, so that Kendal was excluded but Cartmel, Furness and Lonsdale were included and grouped together as Lonsdale hundred. Topographically, Lonsdale meant 'the valley of the Lune' and was used to define places within that area, but in administrative use its sense changed. It has become customary to distinguish the Cartmel-Furness section, William I's grant to Roger, as 'Lonsdale North of the Sands' (i.e. the sands of Morecambe Bay) and the later grant by William II of the more southerly area as 'Lonsdale South of the Sands'. It was this second grant, separating this part of the hundred from the holdings of Ivo Taillebois, lord of Spalding, that determined the county boundaries with Westmoreland and Yorkshire here and left places in those counties still topographically defined as 'Lonsdale'.

The six hundreds of Lancashire have formed a useful organising principle for studies of history and place-names and can justly be said to be earlier than the county itself. It has already been seen that the boundaries of the hundreds of Lonsdale and West Derby were redefined after the Doomsday Survey. There was also a redistribution of townships between the hundreds of Blackburn and Amounderness c1100 which changed the boundaries of those hundreds. Hence, the boundaries were not ancient or fixed, and they certainly do not necessarily follow the physical features which determined the patterns of settlement or were recognised as significant.

Districts There are a number of names for areas not recognised in these standard administrative divisions. Each of the two peninsulas in Lonsdale North of the Sands together with its hinterland has its own name; Cartmel takes its name from that of its major township, the manor called Cherchebi in the Doomsday Survey, while Furness takes its name from a headland which must subsequently have been re-named — perhaps Rampside Point. Further south, the large peninsula between the coast and the Preston-Lancaster road is called The Fylde, 'plain', because of its predominantly flat landscape. Other names for large topographical divisions include Bowland and Rossendale, both assimilated to administrative application through the establishment of forest-areas (see below); both present problems for the place-name scholar, but Rossendale is particularly interesting because of its implications for Celtic settlement. South of the R. Ribble, the names Makerfield and Lyne both perhaps suggest early administrative and/or territorial areas. The reader is referred to the directory for a discussion of all these names, but it may here be noted that some of the difficulties in interpreting them arise from the fact that they have no continuity in the later administrative divisions of the county but are retained either as useful topographical indicators or as conventional additions to common names.

Forest In the Middle Ages the forest was an important territorial and administrative unit. Today this French loan-word suggests to us a large and heavily wooded region, but for the Middle Ages it had administrative importance; it meant the area where the forest law obtained. The forest laws were designed to preserve the animals which the king wished to hunt. They prohibited ordinary people from killing the deer and boar, from keeping dogs which might kill them, from destroying their food, from turning deer pasture into arable land. Areas under these laws were not necessarily heavily wooded throughout, but were places where game-animals could be found. The surrounding area, the purlieu of the forest, was also placed under these laws as a deterrent to poachers. Settlement in and development of such areas was limited by this legislation, which was enforced by special forest courts, so that development is much slower than in other parts of the county. Some technical distinction must be observed between the 'forest', held by the king; the 'chase', from OFr. chacier, 'to hunt', which was a forest-area in which the king allowed his hunting-rights to be transferred to a private individual; and the 'park', from OFr. parc, referring to an enclosed area exempt from forest law if it was in private hands, even if it lay within the forest.

Although the idea of a forest area where hunting-rights were preserved by law was familiar in late Anglo-Saxon England, it was the Normans who established a system of forest-laws separate from the laws for the rest of the country. The areas covered by such laws change from time to time, but it may be helpful to indicate the main areas of demesne forest and chase in the county. In the south-west were the parks of Toxteth and Croxteth and the areas of Burtonwood and Simonswood. More extensive forest lay further north, in Rossendale, Trawden and Pendle. North of the Ribble were the smaller forests of Fulwood and Myerscough and the vast area of forest covering Roeburndale, Quernmore, Over Wyresdale and Bleasdale. Most of these had probably been under Anglo-Saxon game laws. When, in the early twelfth century, the de Lacy family, who held the honour of Clitheroe, were given the right of free chase and warren throughout Blackburnshire and Chippingdale, a large area of hunting land in Yorkshire was added to the forest land of Lancaster, including the chases of Bowland and Blackburn.

The existence of large tracts of forest influenced settlement and economic development, both within the forests and also in the townships within the purlieu of the forest. A case in point is the forest of Blackburn hundred, which was disforested only in 1507. Here there had been development in the Middle Ages for, before 1305, all the deer had been confined to the parks at Ightenhill and Musbury and Henry de Lacy, lord of the honour of Clitheroe, had encouraged cattle farming in the forest areas. In Pendle, many of the modern townships, such as Old Laund Booth or Goldshaw Booth, still preserve ODan. *bōth*, 'dairyman's hut, cattle shelter', which recalls their origins as medieval dairy farms or vaccaries. In Rossendale, a different pattern emerged as the large dairy farms gave way to smaller pastoral farms after disforestation, and the economy and development of the region were later affected further by the introduction of the textile industry. In both Pendle and Rossendale, late economic development was matched by a new and late parochial division, suggested by names such as Newchurch-in-Pendle and Newchurch-in-Rossendale.

Village, Manor, Parish   The majority of entries in the directory refer to hamlets, villages or townships. These settlements were in origin economic, and the most important was the village. Most villages develop in the Anglo-Saxon period as communes to clear the woodland, farm the land − often in large common fields − graze their cattle, provide mutual security. The village would exploit the land around it and would gain rights to that land. Sometimes the link between a community and the lands it held is still preserved in modern names, as in Dalton Lees or Hale and Halewood. It may be assumed that in many cases, where the name of a settlement is also applied to a neighbouring moor, moss, wood, or fell, the settlement had rights within that area and that it fell within the township. The name Threaphaw Fell possibly indicates a summit on which the rights of different townships came into conflict. Neighbourhood and ownership thus go together, which may explain why in some instances, such as Billington and Shevington, the names of neighbouring features are preserved in the name of the township but have otherwise disappeared; the features are more effectively identified by proximity to a village and by ownership than by topographical description.

These settlements, founded upon and sustained by a collective economy, form part of a wider administrative system. One element in this system is the 'manor', a French word meaning 'house, mansion' but more widely

21

applied to the territory under the authority of a lord of the manor within the feudal system. The names Trafford and Stretford reflect a situation in which two forms of the same name have survived to distinguish the township of Stretford from the manor which was formed from it. Such reflections of the manorial system in modern place-names are rare, but the manor and its lord were important. Sometimes the names of the families appear as defining elements in place-names, as in Yealand Conyers and Yealand Redmayne or Charnock Richard, indicating the lord of the manor within which the township lies — the name of the township being, of course, much older than the name of the family. Not infrequently the manor, having no basis in economic development, has disappeared or, as with West Derby, become so insignificant that we have difficulty in understanding why anyone should have wished to distinguish it from the county town of Derbyshire. But the history of many townships includes periods of dispute about matters in which the interests of the lord of the manor and those of the townspeople were at variance.

A second administrative system including the townships was the system of parishes. The origins of this system lay in the ecclesiastical division of the county into townships or groups of townships, each with its own church and priest to whom tithes and other dues were paid. Because of the historical circumstances of the Anglo-Saxon period, the parishes of Lancashire after the Norman Conquest were under the authority of two different dioceses — Lichfield for the area south of the R. Ribble through its deanery at Chester, and York for the area north of the Ribble. From the parochial system developed the system of civil parishes which provided the basis of much local administration and survived into the system of local parish councils. The division of Lancashire into ecclesiastical parishes has taken a more expansive course as new parishes have been created in towns and suburbs to serve the growing populations, and today the word 'parish' is most likely to raise associations which are not primarily administrative.

The parishes of Lancashire in the Middle Ages, like its hundreds, were unusually large. Camden, writing in the late sixteenth century, found 'parishes 36 and no more' and commented that 'for multitude of inhabitants (they) farre exceed the greatest parishes elsewhere'. Before the Reformation, only nine parishes consisted of a single township — Aughton, Claughton, Halton, Heysham, Lytham, Pennington, Radcliffe, Tatham and Whittington — while Whalley, the largest parish in Lancashire, included thirty townships. These large divisions probably attest the early poverty of Lancashire and its sparse population, although from the end of the fifteenth century the county quickly catches up with the rest of the country. Theoretically, these large parishes could involve villagers in long journeys to church in bad weather, over inhospitable countryside, but in practice chapels of ease like the two Newchurch's already mentioned were set up, and in time these developed into parishes in their own right. Some few chapels developed from the private chantry chapels of the lords of the manor. Place-names offer valuable evidence about the church in Lancashire before the Norman Conquest. Place-names which contain words meaning 'church', such as Brit. *eclēsia*, OE *cirice* and ON *kirkja*, are indicative of churches of pre-Conquest foundation – in the case of *eclēsia*, of Celtic foundation. We may therefore infer that there were churches at Cartmel (Cherchebi DB), Church, Churchtown (in Kirkland), Eccles, Eccleshill, Eccleston, Kirkby, Kirkdale (the church was at Walton), Kirkland, Lancaster (Chercaloncastre DB), Ormskirk and St. Michael's-on-Wyre (Michelescherce DB); some instances of OE *prēost*, 'priest', seen in Prescot, Preston and Prestwich, may suggest a pre-Conquest foundation. It is tempting to include here names which contain OIr *cros*, introduced by the converted Norwegian settlers from Ireland as ON *kross*, 'cross', and its equivalent in OE, *rōd*, 'rood'; there are early crosses at certain Lancashire churches and it was a practice in the early period to set up preaching crosses. But 'cross' could refer to a cross marking a boundary or a meeting-place, and 'rood' could even be used of a gibbet. However, the reference to a church at Croston in 1092 which must have been of pre-Conquest foundation perhaps suggests the sense of 'preaching cross' for that name, and the possibility cannot be completely excluded for Crosby and Crossens.

In this way, place-names complement the evidence of archaeology and historical record. The evidence must, however, be used with caution since not all 'church-reference' names are old. Churchtown, Southport, is the modern name of North Meols. St. Helens takes its name from a sixteenth-century chapel of ease, like the Newchurch examples already quoted. St. Annes takes its name from a church built only in the nineteenth century. The later chapelries were usually set up in places which had been in existence for some time before and had already been identified by reference to some feature other than a church.

At this point it is helpful to reconsider the meaning of 'township'. The village is the important element in the township. It is usually held to be distinguished from the 'hamlet', a French word meaning 'little home', not only because it is bigger, but also because it has a church. By this latter definition there would be few villages in Norman Lancashire. But not all townships were in origin villages; they might be a grouping of a number of scattered houses or groups of houses (i.e. hamlets) in an area, no less communal in activity but lacking any nucleus. Probably there was never a village at Eccleshill or Extwistle; both survive and are recorded in the directory as parish-names – the latter as part of Briercliffe-with-Extwistle and in the name Extwistle Moor. The parish of Bispham has the minor name of Bispham Hall, but there is no village. In some cases, the original village has disappeared, as at Samlesbury, one of the most important vills of Blackburn hundred, where very little settlement survives today around the church; the name survives as the parish name, but here, in addition, as the name of a later industrial settlement at Samlesbury Bottoms.

The depopulation of Lancashire villages has not, so far as the present author is aware, been studied in any detail and its causes often cannot be precisely determined. In some cases one can only speculate that the cause was economic, as perhaps with the village of Great Mearley, still in existence in the early sixteenth century but reduced today to a few houses — Mearley survives in the parish name, and in the minor name of Little Mearley Hall. In some cases the cause may have been a visitation of plague, which is known to have hit the county badly from time to time. Coastal erosion or deposit removed a number of villages, such as Argarmeles in West Derby hundred and Fordbottle and Hert in Amounderness hundred. Hapton and Birtwistle disappear in the sixteenth century, soon after permission was given, in about 1514, to Sir John Towneley to enclose his fields at those places, and the cause there may be inferred to have been the economic consequences of this improvement by the lord of the manor. Birtwistle has disappeared completely; Hapton survived as a parish name and developed again as an industrial centre. The latter, however, serves to remind us that continuity of name does not necessarily imply continuity of settlement. When the monks of Kirkstall Abbey improved the farming of their Lancashire lands, they completely depopulated the vill of Accrington and probably also the vill of Cliviger (although Cliviger was quickly resettled). The reader should recognise the precarious nature of community life in early Lancashire and be conscious of the effects which this has had upon the names which have survived into modern use and the way in which they have survived.

Names which survive only as parish or minor names provide particular problems, because the transfer of a name from a township to a parish may be late and the features referred to in the name will be those of the township, not those of the parish. Without knowing the exact site of the settlement, it may be difficult to decide which hill or marsh or similar feature is intended, or even which etymology should be preferred. Modern minor names may be helpful, but one cannot always be sure that they are near the settlement site and have not taken the name of the neighbouring lost settlement at a late date. The problem is compounded in a parish without nucleated settlement, where the name may well be a district name to which any one of a number of features may have contributed.

Final evidence of the poverty of early Lancashire is provided by the fact that, in Doomsday Survey, no land in the county was held by a religious house. A number of religious houses were, of course, founded in the county during the Middle Ages, and land within Lancashire came into the possession of houses outside the county, such as Kirkstall Abbey already mentioned. Yet these developments were generally too late to be reflected in the county's names. A major exception was the foundation of a daughter house of Furness Abbey, the Abbey of Wyresdale, which was begun but later abandoned. The temporary buildings would have been removed and would be unlikely to leave much trace for an archaeologist, but within the Wyresdale area the name 'Abbeystead' appears as both a major and a minor name and it may be assumed that one of the sites bearing this name was the original site of Wyresdale Abbey. A second exception is the name Grange, reflecting the system whereby the monks set up an outlying farm to cultivate the lands which had been given to the house but which were distant from it.

Beyond these few examples, religious houses contribute little towards the creation of names, but their detailed records and accounts provide invaluable evidence of early place-names, and the enterprise shown by their members in developing the agriculture and mineral wealth of the county in the Middle Ages contributed to the later pattern of settlement. Of the houses in Lancashire, only the site of Cockersand Abbey has never been re-settled; the name is included in the directory for its historical associations.

The development of administrative systems in Lancashire was slow. The county was poor and its administrative units were large. Yet ultimately it is upon the records of the various administrative divisions here considered that we depend for the bulk of our evidence of Lancashire place-names.

3 Topography

Lancashire South of the Sands may conveniently be divided into two kinds of landscape running north-south. The first of these is the upland landscape, including all the land to the east of the county. This part of Lancashire has no mountains but only moorlands, flat-topped and peat-covered. The hills are divided by steep valleys with rivers or streams. This upland landscape, which includes most of the forest-areas discussed earlier, presented considerable problems for settlement and development. For an agricultural economy, dairy-farming was the most appropriate activity in these regions and the characteristic settlement-pattern was a series of small farms and upland summer pastures. In the early period of the Industrial Revolution, however, the water-power provided by the rivers led to the development of the textile industry in the southern valleys, particularly those just north of Manchester. The nature of the landscape dictated the form of these textile villages, their houses built, often in local stone, around the factory and extending along the valley and to a limited degree

25

up the hillsides. Here, as with the earlier farms, the effect remains one of isolated and self-contained communities.

The second kind of landscape is the lowland landscape which consists of the land of 400 feet and below. This area of plain extends inland from the coast and forms a kind of triangle whose base extends across the Mersey-Irwell system and whose apex is north of Lancaster. This landscape includes much of the land south of the R. Ribble, and also the Fylde. It ends in the west at the coast, an area of sand-hills or salt-marsh whose shape has constantly changed through erosion and deposit by the sea. It is bounded in the east by the upland landscape. This lowland area contained much marshland and a number of rivers and streams which were always liable to flood. For the early settlers the problem was to find firm, well-drained land where they could practise arable farming. Engineering developments have made possible the draining of many of the old marsh-areas and the control of the rivers, and have therefore made us less conscious of the physical obstacles confronting the early settlers. Moreover, the plain-area also contains the south Lancashire coalfield, an important source of power for the Industrial Revolution, as well as having, or being near, other major raw materials for industrial processes and being better situated than the uplands for the development of communications with the rest of the country and, through the ports of Lancaster, Preston, and particularly Liverpool (with Manchester as a later development), with the rest of the world. Hence the coalfield area south of the Ribble has witnessed a growth in industry and population from the early nineteenth-century and has come to stand in many minds as a picture of the whole county. These industrial towns, unlike those of the uplands, were not physically restricted by the topography but were free to spread across the plain, joining up finally to form great continuous conurbations in which the original identity of villages and townships has been lost. Whereas the villages of the uplands tend to be built of the local stone, the towns of the lowlands are of brick, and later concrete.

The Cartmel and Furness peninsulas north of the Sands, separated from the rest of Lancashire by Westmorland and by the expanse of Morecombe Bay, do not fit this simple pattern. Cartmel's coast consists mainly of low land and reclaimed salt-marsh and further arable land is found along the broad valley of the R. Eea; the rest is limestone hills. The area developed mainly as an agricultural region, particularly in the seventeenth century. Furness, on the other hand, consists of two different landscapes – the mountains of High Furness, the only true mountains of the county, and the limestone hills of Low or Plain Furness which come down to the sea. These limestone hills contain iron ore which was exploited by the monks of Furness Abbey and which, more recently, was the basis of the industrial development of Barrow and the growth of the ports of

Ulverston and Barrow.

This simplified picture of Lancashire can be modified still further. First, the distinction between western lowland and eastern upland must be related to the division of the county by its great rivers. At the time of the Anglo-Saxon settlement and for long afterwards any waterway potentially served a dual function. It could provide a useful and quick means of communication in what must have been primitive, shallow-draught vessels. Thus, today it is difficult to imagine a landing place on the R. Alt as the name Huyton suggests, because we think in terms of road-transport and because the nature of the landscape has changed. But rivers, and even quite small streams, also presented barriers to communication. Their crossing-points are marked by names in *ford*, such as Rufford or Rainford; by later names in *bridge*, such as Newby Bridge, where *bridge* has been added to an older name, or Penny Bridge which takes its name from the family who built the bridge on the site of a former ford; or in names which indicate a ferry, as in Hollinfare, the former name of Hollins Green, or Fiddlers Ferry — records sometimes use the word *boat* after a place-name, as in Salesbury Boat, to indicate a ferry-crossing. But some rivers in their lower reaches presented particular and permanent difficulties for crossing. The R. Mersey, the 'boundary river', is still the county boundary; it is unusual in bearing an Anglo-Saxon rather than a Celtic name, and was probably re-named by the Anglo-Saxons when it became the boundary between the kingdoms of Mercia and Northumbria. In isolating the land between Ribble and Mersey, Doomsday Survey not only reflected the territorial and administrative importance of the Mersey but also confirmed that the R. Ribble has a similar importance. Critics who have studied the dialects of Middle English tend to agree that somewhere in this area is the transition-point between the North-west Midland and Northern dialects — the R. Ribble has frequently been claimed to form this division, although certain feature-differences have also been tentatively located along the Lune and even along the Douglas. These differences of opinion reflect the small amount of precisely dated and located material needed for the study of dialect in this area, and also perhaps the fact that dialect-boundaries are always shifting as populations move and communication becomes easier. However, this area was contested between Mercia and Northumbria before 600, and the division of ecclesiastical responsibility between York for the land north of the Ribble and Lichfield for land south provides further evidence of the topographical, administrative and linguistic importance of the great rivers as east-west divisions (see Section 4, pp.34).

A second modification may be made by reference to the settlement-patterns discussed in section 4. Norwegian settlement tends to follow the area along the coastal strip while Danish settlement is in the eastern uplands and the neighbouring parts of the plain. The further north one goes, the greater the area of upland and the greater the concentration of Norse names; in the peninsulas north of the Sands such names are heavily concentrated. Thus there is some correlation between topography and Norse settlement, and this is reflected in the kind of words used – relating to hills, rocks, crags etc. and to dairy farming. It is probably no coincidence that these areas are among the less attractive places to settle and might well have been available for new development at the time of Norse settlement.

The remainder of this section will attempt to show how the topography just discussed is reflected in the place-names. However, it is important to remember that place-names provide only limited evidence of topography. Not all names refer to features of the landscape or to their agricultural consequences, and those that do usually attempt to show what is distinctive about a place rather than what it has in common with other places nearby. For example, the name Clayton, which is found in three major names so close together that they require distinguishing additions, means not only that these three farms or enclosures were on clay soil but that the soil was distinctively different from that on other farms in the area – otherwise there would be no point in using it as a distinctive reference. On the other hand, a simple toponymic, such as Holme, or a name in which the topographical reference is clearly not the main distinctive point, as in Arley, 'clearing for ploughing', does provide information of a more general kind.

Marshland   The lowland area contained a large number of marshy areas called *mosses*. South of the R. Ribble, the largest of these was Martin Mere, 'the biggest meare in Lancashire, three miles in length and two in breadth' as Leland described it. Adjoining it was Halsall Moss, with Rainford and Knowsley Mosses further west and Chat Moss and Trafford Moss nearer Manchester. In the Fylde were the mosses of Marton, Pilling, Rawcliffe and Stalmine, a major factor in isolating the Fylde as a region from the rest of the county. Much of this land was reclaimed for agriculture in the late eighteenth-earlier nineteenth centuries. Rainford Moss, for example, was drained in the 1780's, Pilling Moss in the 1830's and Martin Mere in a number of projects between 1692 and 1813. It has been estimated that in the eighteenth century there were 34,500 acres of mossland in the county, compared with 4,500 acres in 1931-32, and that does not include the boggy land and water-meadows beside the rivers and streams which were always liable to flood.

The usual words for these areas are 'moss' and 'marsh', both OE in origin and usually added to an existing place-name. The former, OE *mēos*, is seen as a first element in such names as Moss Bank, Mossborough, Mossley, Moss Side, and Moston while the latter, OE *mersc*, is seen in Marshaw. The first element of Martin and Marton is OE *mere*, 'pool', although this must be distinguished from OE *(ge)mǣre*, 'boundary', in modern names. In Scandinavian areas, ON *mýrr*, 'mire', and *kjarr*, 'boggy land covered with brushwood', are more usual, as in Myerscough, Altcar and Hoscar. OE *fennig*, 'muddy', is seen in Feniscliffe and Feniscowles, both on the R. Darwen. OE **lǣc (c)*, 'stream, bog', is the source of the stream-name Leck and still survives in dialect *lache*, 'stream flowing through boggy land'.

Other words suggest higher, dry land in marshland. PrWelsh **inis*, Welsh *ynys* means 'island' but in Ince and Inskip it seems to have the sense of either 'water-meadow' or 'dry ground'. A similar range is found for OE *ēg*, 'island', which is seen perhaps only in The Eyes in Lancashire major-names but which Ekwall notes as of frequent occurrence in field-names. ON *holmr*, ODan. *hulm* also means 'island' in the sense of 'water-meadow' and 'dry ground amidst marshes', as in Levenshulme. Both *ēg* and *holmr* are found in the modern sense of 'island' also, as, for example, in the North Lonsdale island names of Fouldray, Foulney, Roa, Walney and Dunnerholme.

A number of words refer to land beside rivers. One of the most common is OE *halh*, which usually means 'nook or corner of land' but often in Lancashire refers to low-lying land beside a river, or by the side of mossland, as in Halsall, Maghull, Ordsall or Rossall. This is one of the most frequently found Lancashire elements and its meaning is more fully discussed in section 5.

Rivers and Streams   Many of the river- and stream-names are Celtic in origin and the antiquity of the name is an indication of their continuing importance. The usual OE words for streams and rivers are OE *burna*, as in Blackburn where the town preserves the river-name whereas the river is now called the Blackwater; OE *wella*, 'well, spring, stream', as in Childwall and Halliwell; and OE *brōc*, which seems to have replaced *burna*, but is more usual as a later addition, as in Gore Brook, than as part of a major name in its own right, as in Tarbock. In Scandinavian areas, ON *bekkr*, 'beck, stream', is more usual, as in Cant Beck and Grizebeck. OE *ēa*, 'river, stream', is not so frequent in Lancashire major names, although it is seen in Mersey and the place-name Ewood and may explain the difficult river-name Eea; its ON equivalent, *á*, is seen in the river-names Greeta and Brathay. OE *wæter* may refer to a river, as in Pendle Water, but in the north-west it can also refer to a lake, as in Hawes Water.

Beside these common forms are others which may seem more unusual. OE **lǣc*, 'bog, stream', has already been noted, ON *kelde*, 'spring, marshy place', is seen in Kellet and although OE *sīc*, ON *sik* is not attested in any of the modern major names, it is frequent in minor names — the word has the sense from OE of 'a small stream, especially one in flat marshland' and from ON of 'a ditch, trench', but it develops the sense of 'field or meadow beside a stream'; it often takes the form *such* in modern names. Here perhaps should also be noted the common northern word, OE *twisla*, 'fork of a river, junction of two streams', seen as first element in Twiss Green and Twiston and as second element in Oswaldtwistle, Entwistle and Extwistle. As with *sīc*, the word seems to refer not only to the junction of the streams but to the land at this point also. A similar sense may perhaps be claimed for OE *tunge*, ON *tunga*, 'tongue of land', which in Icelandic has the sense of 'tongue of land at the junction of two rivers', which would fit the location of Tonge. Two other terms unfamiliar to us today are OE *pēote*, 'torrent, fountain, water-conduit, pipe', in Thatto Heath, and OE *lād*, 'watercourse, passage over a river', in Oglet. Finally, it should be noted that OE *lacu*, like modern dialect *lake*, had the sense of 'stream, watercourse', as in Medlock.

Four other 'water-words' should also be noted. Modern *lake* appears in Middle English, from Latin *lacus*, in the sense of 'lake, pool'. In Scandinavian areas, ON *tjǫrn*, 'tarn, lake', is preferred, as in Tarn Hows. OE *pōl* has the sense not only of 'pond' as in Poulton but also of 'pool in a river' and 'creek', as in Liverpool and Skippool. ON *fors*, OWScand. *foss*, 'waterfall', again surviving in dialect form, *force*, is found in some names from the Scandinavian area such as Force and Skelwith Force.

While this account does not cover the range of Celtic names and gives only a sample of the frequency of many of the elements, the diversity of words may well seem surprising today. Although this diversity is partly explained by the fact that three languages have contributed to the stock, it also reflects both the diversity of terms within Old English and also the special words and even special senses which develop. Above all, the terms reflect a concern with water for settlement, agriculture, communication and life itself which, in the age of the North-West Water Authority, we have lost.

Forest and Woodland   Beside the drainage of the mossland, the clearance of the woodland must rank as the major development in Lancashire. Place-names still preserve references to woodland, of which the most obvious is OE *wudu*, 'wood', as in the former forest-areas of Simonswood and Burtonwood. Other words include Brit. **cēto*, 'wood', with some later word appended, as in Cheetham, the tautologous Cheetwood and Culcheth; and ON *skógr*, 'wood', as in Burscough, Tarlscough and Cunscough. A very common element in Lancashire, however, is OE *sceaga*, 'small wood, copse, strip of undergrowth or wood', which survives in the dialect word *shaw*, 'strip of undergrowth surrounding a field'. The element is found in many names, major and minor, such as Shaw, Birtenshaw, Crawshaw and Bradshaw. Other OE words include *bearu*, 'wood, grove', as in Bare and Barrow (although this must be carefully distinguished from OE *beorg*, 'hill'); *grǣfe*, grove, copse, thicket', in the form *greave*, as in Ramsgreave, another element particularly common in Lancashire, as opposed to OE *grāf* which has the same sense; and *hyrst*, 'hillock, copse', where the sense of woodland is only one possibility but is clear in Nuthurst. ON *lúndr*, 'grove', is found in Lunt.

While these names provide evidence of woodland, they also suggest places where woodland may have been distinctive. A better guide to the large area of woodland in the county is provided by elements which suggest clearings. The element most frequently cited in this connection is OE *lēah*, and in many cases it probably does suggest a man-made clearing in woodland, particularly where it is combined with a personal name, as in Mawdesley or Knowsley. However, as the discussion of this element in section 5 indicates, *lēah* had a wide range of meanings, including any kind of cleared land and also any naturally formed woodland glade, and its evidence should therefore be interpreted with caution. In Scandinavian areas, ON *þveit*, 'clearing, meadow, paddock', also suggests an area of cleared woodland, as in Hawthwaite or Langthwaite. Legal documents sometimes refer to 'rod land', from OE **rod, *rodu*, 'a clearing', an element which is particularly common in Lancashire minor names, such as Roddecroft, as well as in such major names as Blackrod and Ormerod; it may also take the forms *royd* and *rote*. Another term for clearing which is common in minor names but is not attested in major names is OE **rydding*, as in the lost name Aremetridding, 'hermit's clearing', near Leyland.

The process of clearing the woodland was necessarily piecemeal and tended to involve individual enterprise. In the forest-areas it was particularly delayed by the restrictions of the forest-laws (see section 2). The result has tended to be a pattern of isolated farmsteads and hamlets with their small fields, linked by a network of country lanes, the kind of pattern seen, for example, in the area of the Pendle Forest. The place-name evidence given above can therefore be correlated both with a certain kind of landscape today and also particularly with the former forest areas.

Hills and Valleys   The usual term for a hill is OE *hyll*. The 'y' in this form indicates a rounded vowel (see section 1) which may be unrounded to 'i', as in standard 'hill', but which in this area, particularly the southern part, remained rounded to 'u', as in Hulton. The element may occur finally, when it is often reduced by weak stress, as in Pendle or Windle.

There were, however, many other words available to describe higher land of one sort or another, and these words may well vary in reference from the lowland area, where they may refer to a slight rise of fifty feet or so in some otherwise flat country such as the Fylde, to the upland area, where they may refer to high hills and peaks. Among the commonest of these are OE *hōh*, 'spur of land', as in Houghton or Clougha, which may mean anything from 'a projecting piece of land' to 'a steep ridge' and, in dialect use, even 'a steep glen'; and, in Scandinavian areas, ON *haugr*, 'hill,

31

burial mound', as in Hackinsall — without early evidence it is often hard to distinguish the two words, and it is equally difficult to determine the exact reference in a number of cases. OE *hlāw, hlǣw,* 'hill, burial mound', is seen in Lowton or Horelaw, and OE *hrycg,* 'ridge', in Foulridge and Longridge. Both OE *hēafod,* 'head, headland, hill' and ON *hǫfuð,* 'head, promontory', are found — the former in, for example, Micklehead, and the latter in Hawkshead. In the upland area both OE *mōr,* 'moor', with the particular sense of 'hill, high moorland', and ON *fjall,* 'fell, mountain' are frequent, as in Quernmore and Hampsfell. OE *dūn,* 'hill, expanse of hill country', has a wide range of meaning from a gentle slope to a high mountain, seen in Hameldown and Downham. Finally, particular reference should be made to Brit. **penno-,* 'hill', which is usually found in combination with OE elements — a fact probably indicating that the Anglo-Saxons did not understand it as a word but accepted it as a hill-name — as in Pemberton, Penwortham and the tautologous Pendle where OE *hyll* has been added.

References to valleys are naturally most frequent in the upland area. In Scandinavian areas, ON *dalr,* 'dale, valley', is the usual word, as in Grisedale. In other areas, OE *denu,* 'valley', is the usual term, as in Deane, Denton and Standen. Because of settlement patterns, *dalr* is found in north Lancashire while *denu* is mainly in the southern part of the county. OE *botm,* 'a valley bottom', is seen in such names as Ramsbottom, a name which has gained comic overtones because of the restriction of the second element in modern usage to an anatomical application; the ON cognate *botn,* 'the head of a valley', is evidenced in Botton. Other words belonging to the upland area include OE *clōh,* 'ravine', as in Clougha; OWScand. *gil,* 'ravine', a word common in the north-west and restricted to areas of Norwegian settlement, as in Ragill; and OWScand. *slakki,* 'shallow valley', another Norwegian term, as in Slack. Two more technical words are OE *hop,* originally meaning 'a plot of enclosed land', but by Middle English developing the sense of 'small enclosed valley', as in Hope, a development perhaps arising from ON *hóp,* 'inlet, bay'; and ON *grein,* originally 'branch of a tree' and 'fork of a stream', but in the name Haslingden Grain referring to a small valley forking off a larger one, a sense also preserved in the dialect word *grain.*

The Coast   The coastal area was not a hospitable region for settlement. The sand-dunes of the coast are reflected in the ON elements *melr,* 'sand-bank', 'sand hill', as in North Meols, and ON *haugr,* as in Hawes. OE *hēafod,* in the sense 'headland', is joined by OE **nes,* ON *nes,* 'headland', as in Crossens and Widnes.

At the right state of the tide it was possible to travel across the sands of Morecambe Bay between the northern and southern parts of Lonsdale. The popularity of this potentially dangerous route, which involves crossing the rivers Kent, Keer and Leven, can be appreciated when it is recalled that the turnpike route to Ulverston was via Kendal. The importance of Morecambe Bay sands can be seen in such names as Grange-over-Sands and Bolton-le-Sands.

Settlement and Agriculture   The pattern of fields with their fences, banks or hedges is of comparatively late development in Lancashire, beginning in places such as Furness perhaps as early as the twelfth century but mostly dating from the late fourteenth to the sixteenth centuries. By this process the large open fields surrounding villages, and also the estates of private landowners, were progressively enclosed. But the process is generally too late to be reflected in the major place-names. When place-names suggest enclosure, they probably refer to a single house and the area surrounding it – i.e. a homestead. Many of these homesteads later develop into larger villages.

The commonest element suggesting such enclosure is OE *tūn*, which, as section 5 indicates, had a wide range of meanings from 'enclosure' to 'village'. Other common words are OE *croft*, 'a small enclosed field', as in Martinscroft, OE *haga*, 'a hedge, enclosure', as in Hawcoate and Haigh, and OE *worð*, 'enclosure', as in Edgeworth. OE *pearroc*, 'fence enclosing a piece of ground', is seen in Parrox and may well have influenced the meaning of some instances of OF *parc*, which usually meant 'enclosed land for game-animals'. While OE *æcer,* as in Linacre, suggests 'a plot of arable land', *feld* has the sense of 'open country', later 'enclosed land for cultivation, the common field', and develops its modern sense of 'enclosed field' only from the fourteenth century.

The upland areas, as already noted, were used for dairy farming and had a large Scandinavian population. Here are found such words as ODan. *bōth,* OWScand. *búð,* 'cattle house'; ON *erg,* 'shieling, hill-pasture', as in Anglezarke; ON *sætr,* 'mountain pasture, shieling', as in Satterthwaite; and Icel. *snap,* 'poor pasture', often hard to distinguish from OE *snæp,* 'boggy land', as in Snape. Villages occupied by the Scandinavians often bear the element *þorp,* 'secondary settlement'. OE *wīc,* 'dairy farm', later 'hamlet, village', is found particularly in the south-eastern part of the county where the evidence suggests that there were fewer Scandinavians – e.g. Prestwich.

References to specific crops and agricultural practices should be interpreted with caution since again the reference is intended to be distinctive. Names such as Barnacre, 'barley field', or Royley, 'clearing where rye is grown', perhaps indicate that these crops were not usual in those immediate areas. Such a probability is especially strong in the case of Barley and Wheatley in the forest of Pendle, an area where dairy-farming was usual and where such grains are not grown today. Conversely, the absence of OE *āte*, 'oats', from major place-names and its relative infrequency in minor names may well suggest that the grain, which Holt

33

in 1795 noted as the county's principal crop, was so common as to be unremarkable. Although it has been suggested that OE *falh* and *felging*, seen in Fallowfield and Falinge, are used in their earlier sense of 'ploughed land' (i.e. land newly broken) rather than in the later sense of 'fallow land', it may be noted that the Lancashire town-fields, unlike those of the Midlands, were rarely left fallow and the later sense might be more immediately distinctive.

It will be evident from this discussion that the problem of the meaning of a name is not necessarily solved when the etymology is determined. The meanings of the words used in Lancashire place-names were not closely limited or definable but were part of the living speech of the time and took their often wide range of meanings from the contexts in which they were used by the local community. Although the OS maps can help us today to recover some of the geographical context to which the words refer, we can only guess at the full range of associations and shades of meaning which many of these words would have had in the various parts of pre-Conquest Lancashire.

4. Patterns of Settlement

Since very little documentary evidence is available for Lancashire in the pre-Conquest period and only limited archaeological evidence — much more may well lie under our modern industrial towns — the historian is compelled to rely mainly on the evidence of place-names for early settlement in the county. Such evidence, however, must be used with care. Very few place-names can be accurately dated — the *-ingas* and *-ingahām* types discussed below are the exceptions. Furthermore, place-names reflect the usage of the majority of people in an area; it is safe to conclude from a number of ON names that there was a majority of Scandinavians in that area, but it is not safe to conclude that there were no Anglo-Saxons also there. The shifting balance of population also results in the replacement of one name by another, and we have no means of deciding how many places which today bear OE or ON names were originally founded and named by Celts. The character of the name may add to our knowledge; the comparative absence of habitational elements in extant Celtic names, or the survival of ON inflections in ON names may suggest a very small Celtic population or a very large and influential Scandinavian population. Occasionally, words or the forms of words are distinctively dialectal and enable us to distinguish, say, the Northumbrian and Mercian areas of the county, or the parts settled by Danes and the parts settled by Norwegians; but again, only a few words provide information of this kind. Finally, names may contain references to Celts or Scandinavians; in such cases the names suggest that the presence of such people was unusual and distinctive and that there were therefore comparatively few Celts or Scandinavians there. In all cases one must remember the nature of place-names and the circumstances under which a name would have been given.

Romano-British Settlement   Place-name elements may well provide clues to earlier prehistoric sites. A particularly interesting example is provided by the names Wharles and Roseacre in the directory, which may refer to the existence of a stone circle or burial mounds. Ancient burial mounds may sometimes be suggested by the elements OE *hlāw*, ON *haugr*, 'mound', and OE *beorg*, 'hill, barrow'. Stone circles may be suggested by OE *hring,* ON *hringr,* 'ring'; OE *hwyrfel,* ON *hvirfill,* 'whorl'; OE *hwēol,* 'wheel'; and ON *kringla,* 'circle'. All these elements are found in Lancashire place-names, especially minor names, and a systematic study would no doubt indicate a large number of sites which warrant archaeological investigation.

However, it is as evidence for settlement from the Romano-British period onwards that place-names are most valuable. The *Geography* of Claudius Ptolomaeus, written in the second century AD, which mentions an occasional place-name (e.g. Morecambe), indicates that Lancashire was in the area of a Celtic tribe called the Brigantes while, to the south, Cheshire was controlled by the Cornovii. The tribal name appears to have developed into a territorial reference, Briganticia, which survived as the name of the Anglo-Saxon kingdom of Bernicia, itself part of the big and once powerful northern kingdom of Northumbria. Lancashire was not of itself important to the Romans, but they built through it two important north-south routes – the first from Chester via Wilderspool, Walton-le-Dale, Lancaster and Overborough, and the second from Chester via Northwich to Manchester, Ribchester and Overborough. East-west routes connected Manchester and Wigan, Ribchester and Kirkham, Lancaster and Brough.

Latin *via strata* 'the paved way', is reflected in OE *strǣt,* 'road', still seen in modern *street*. It provides the first element of Stretford and Trafford, 'the ford on the Roman road'. Not all instances of OE *strǣt* in place-names will refer to Roman roads, but a large number may. The element is not uncommon in minor names, and F.T. Wainwright has drawn attention to its frequency in the field-names of the Fylde, noting that a number of these names may mark the line of the Ribchester-Kirkham road. This road, called 'Danes Pad', has been the subject of much discussion, and Wainwright suggests that the theory of its continuation west of Kirkham may also be supported by the evidence of minor names.

The Roman forts on these roads bore Latin names such as Mamucium (Manchester), Coccium (Wigan) and Bremetennacum (Ribchester), but those names have not survived. In a number of instances, the modern name consists of a word of Celtic origin to which has been added OE *caster* – the form north of the R. Ribble – or *ceaster*, from Latin *castra*, 'camp'. The main examples are Lancaster, Ribchester and Manchester, the first two having Celtic river-names as their first elements.

However, there appears to be some correlation between the system of Roman roads and Roman settlements and the distribution of Celtic place-names. One cluster of Celtic names appears around the Roman settlement of Manchester — Eccles, Pendlebury, Pendleton and Worsley to the west, Cheetham and Cheetwood to the north and Chadderton to the north-east. Roman Coccium today bears a name that may well be Celtic, Wigan, and nearby are the Celtic names of Bryn, Ince and Pemberton to the south, with Kenyon, Culcheth and Glazebury rather further away and Eccleston and Haydock to the south-west; Penketh, another Celtic name, is west of Warrington. Another small group of Celtic names is found further north, nearer Leyland, in Eccleston and Charnock Richard; while Penwortham, with its Celtic first element, is on the R. Ribble. Further Celtic names dot the Fylde, in Great Eccleston, Inskip, Preesall, Preese, Rossall and Treales. Winkley and Dinkley, again with Celtic first elements, are found on the Ribble above Ribchester. The major name Cark and the minor name Blenket are the few examples of Celtic names in Lonsdale North of the Sands.

The Anglo-Saxons also sometimes identified a place as owned or occupied by a Celt. OE *walh*, however, can be used in a variety of senses, including both 'Briton' and 'serf', and it is by no means certain which sense is intended in each case. It is interesting to note that the Roman settlement south of the Ribble was called Walton by the Anglo-Saxons and that Ulnes Walton is near the villages of Eccleston and Charnock already noted. Another Walton is found near Liverpool, more remote from areas of Celtic names and Roman influence, and to the south-east of it is Brettargh Holt, whose first element is ON *Bretar*, from OE *Brettas*, 'Britons'. Possibly the last two suggest areas where it was unusual to find Celts, but the others do seem to correlate with areas in which there was a Celtic population of some size.

Thus, it is possible to claim that there were Celtic settlements in Lancashire. The detailed evidence above can be supported by the large number of Celtic river-names in the county, names not only for large rivers, which tend generally to bear Celtic names throughout the country, but for quite small streams. Makerfield, moreover, seems to be a Celtic district-name in origin and refers to the Wigan area where there is a concentration of Celtic place-names. Furthermore, most of the names occur in the area south of the Ribble and the places bearing them lie between 100 and 500 feet, on the higher ground in the lowland area. Although it is often claimed that the Celts were exterminated or driven into the hills by the Anglo-Saxon invaders, the evidence of place-names in Lancashire does not support that conclusion.

On the other hand, the character of the names does not suggest that there was a particularly close contact between the Celts and the Anglo-Saxons. Only Treales refers to any habitation. All the others refer to natural features, such as hills or woods, and the form of the name often indicates that the Anglo-Saxons did not understand Celtic. Names such as Pendle or Cheetwood, where the OE element has the same meaning as the Celtic element, seem to suggest that *penno-* and *cēto-* were regarded as names rather than as meaningful words. Both Kenyon and Wigan would seem to represent personal names surviving from a phrasal construction, and some simple forms such as Bryn and Ince may formerly have been part of extended constructions. It seems probable that some of the difficulties in interpreting names of Celtic origin may arise from the corruption of the Celtic names on the lips of the Anglo-Saxons.

Anglo-Saxon Settlement   The Anglo-Saxon settlement of England is usually said to begin in the second half of the fifth century, but settlers probably arrived in Lancashire long after that date. Documentary evidence is slight but important. It is recorded that King Æthelfrith of Northumbria (the Anglo-Saxon kingdom to the east and north) advanced against the Britons in the west, first defeating them in the battle of Degsastan in 603 and thereby separating Lancashire from the Celtic kingdom of Strathclyde, and then advancing south to Chester where he won a further decisive victory some time between 613 and 616. The Northumbrian conquest of Lancashire is further confirmed by the fact that Eadwine, Æthelfrith's successor, conquered the offshore islands of Man and Anglesey. It is also said that King Ecgfrith of Northumbria (670-85) gave to St. Cuthbert Cartmel and all the British with it, which indicates both Northumbrian supremacy in North Lonsdale and also the existence of a subject Celtic population there.

Three types of place-name formation are cited as evidence of early settlement. The first is the place-name formed by combining an OE personal name with the suffix *-ingas.* As the *-as* plural ending suggests, these place-names are strictly folk-names and belong to a period at which the main allegiance was not to a place but to a tribe or family; the exact reference may be debatable, but 'the people associated with' the person bearing the personal name of the first element is a reasonable practical translation. Such names are found almost exclusively in areas of early settlement, usually in places which are readily accessible and might have been particularly attractive to early settlers, and the places bearing the names have often retained their importance to the present time. As the discussion of *-ingas* in section 5 below suggests, however, it is often difficult on the comparatively late evidence of Lancashire forms to be certain that modern names in *-ing* do go back to this folk-form and not to a suffix *-ing* which has different meanings and may remain productive for a much longer period. The Lancashire names which may show the *-ingas*

37

ending are Bryning, Staining and two examples each of Melling and Billinge. The reader is referred to the discussion of these names in the directory, but it may be noted that Melling would appear to be the most probable example of this ending.

The second type of early place-name formation shows the combination of an OE personal name with the possessive form of the *-ingas* suffix and the word for 'homestead, community', resulting in the ending *-ingahām*, which could be translated 'home of the people associated with' the person bearing the personal name which forms the first element. This type of name arose slightly later than the first examples of the *-ingas* form and continued rather longer, so that *-ingahām* forms are found in areas where there are also *-ingas* forms but additionally in areas beyond, where there are no *-ingas* forms. There are four possible examples of this type of name in Lancashire — Aldingham, Habergham, Padiham and Whittingham.

The third, and more questionable, example of an early place-name type is represented by names which have the possessive form of *-ingas* and OE *tūn*, 'farmstead', giving the ending *-ingatūn*. This may be translated 'the farmstead belonging to the people associated with' the person bearing the personal name of the first element. There are several difficulties in interpreting modern *-ington* forms. The first, particularly for Lancashire, is again the absence of early forms which would reflect the important possessive ending '-a-'; the second is the recognised existence of forms which even in OE were *-ingtūn* rather than *-ingatūn* forms and whose first element was not a personal name — forms which are not based on a folk-name and which cannot be said to be early; the third is the continuing productivity of the element *tūn* throughout the Anglo-Saxon period, unlike *hām*, which quickly goes out of use, or *lēah* and *feld*, which belong to a later period of settlement when early sites were being extended. Hence there are usually two considerations to bear in mind when considering names which today end in *-ington*. The first is that only those place-names which have personal names as their first elements could be early; the second is that, of those, only a proportion are likely to be early, but it will be impossible to say exactly which. The possible old *-ington* names are Adlington, Alkrington, Dumplington, Pennington, Pilkington, Pleasington, Tottington; it is tempting to include Warrington, clearly an important crossing-point of the Mersey in Roman times, and Worthington, which is near the cluster of British names round Wigan, but it seems safer to regard them as derived from current words (see directory). Three other *-ington* forms must be regarded with caution — Wennington, which may contain a river-name; Billington, which records show was originally *Billingadūn*, though it is probably an early name; and Whittington, which may well be early but which contains the OE name Hwīta which remained in use throughout the Anglo-Saxon period.

An examination of the distribution of these names shows that none is in the upland area and most are in the higher, better drained land of the lowland area between 100 and 500 feet. Most lie on or near the rivers Lune and Ribble or their tributaries, which might suggest the importance of these rivers in directing and limiting settlement. The exceptions to this are Bryning and Staining in the Fylde, the former not far from the Roman road at Kirkham whose westerly extension has been briefly discussed above, and the latter close to the parish bearing the Celtic name of Preese; it may be significant that the Fylde contains a number of Celtic names, including the name of habitational reference, Treales. A further exception is the isolated coastal settlement in Furness, Aldingham. Some further interesting correlations are the proximity of Padiham and Habergham and the parish of Ightenhill with its Celtic name; and the proximity of Pleasington and Billinge to Mellor, another Celtic name. One might tentatively deduce from this evidence that early settlement tended to follow the river valleys and/or to be in or near areas of existing Celtic settlement; but the very limited amount of evidence available for early settlement in Lancashire makes any generalisation questionable.

Although it is generally agreed that Lancashire was first colonised from Northumbria, it is also agreed that a later colonisation, from Mercia, also took place. The pagan Mercian king Penda (626-55) invaded Northumbria in 633 and perhaps began the colonisation of Lancashire soon after. The land in the West Riding of Yorkshire conquered by Mercia was subsequently regained by Northumbria but its population remained predominantly Mercian. In 829 Northumbria submitted to Egbert, king of Wessex, to take its place in the united Anglo-Saxon kingdom which followed the re-conquest of the Danelaw.

The mixture of Northumbrians and Mercians in the population of the county is reflected in a number of features in the place-names. Two important ones are features of pronunciation or accent. In the Northumbrian area, OE *c* before *æ* represented the initial sound of *cat* whereas in the Mercian area it represented the initial sound of *chat*. Thus, Latin *castra* develops as Mercian *ceaster*, modern *chester*, as in Manchester and Ribchester, but as Northumbrian *cæster*, modern *caster,* as in Lancaster; it is, however, possible that the latter form shows Norse influence, since it is limited to the Danelaw. Latin *cathedra* is seen in PrWelsh **cadeir*, 'chair', which develops as *chadder* in the Mercian area, as in Chadder, Chadderton, Chatterton and Chat Moss, but in more northerly counties develops as *cadder*. The division between the two developments, *c* and *ch*, is along the Ribble valley. Although Ribchester, to the north of the Ribble, has the ch-form today, it was a c-form in the DB entry.

A second feature is the development of OE *æ* before *l* followed by another consonant in certain words which formerly contained *i* or *j* in their second syllable. The Mercian development is _æ_, modern _a_, whereas the Northumbrian is _e_. A common element showing this development is OE _wella_, 'stream'; in the Mercian area it develops as _wall_, as in Childwall and Winewall, while in the Northumbrian area it appears as _well_, as in Wiswell. The form of the element may readily change; thus, Winewall first appears as a _well_-form, as might be expected in an area near the Ribble, while Halliwell, in Salford Hundred, first appears as a _wall_-form. Again, the Ribble valley seems to form the division between the two developments.

Three further important dialect features concern vocabulary. The form _bōðl_, 'dwelling', and _*bōðl-tūn_, 'an enclosure with buildings' are distinctively Northumbrian, and the latter is seen in Bolton, a name found once north of the Ribble and twice south of it; moreover, the chiefly northern form, _bōtl_, is seen in Bootle near Liverpool. The chiefly Mercian form, _bold_, however, is confined to the area south of the Ribble, as in Bold, Newbold and Parbold, and does not appear in the Northumbrian area to the north. A second form is OE _worðign_, 'enclosure', which is typical of the West Midland area. Although particularly common in Shropshire and Herefordshire, it is attested south of the Ribble in a lost name, Faldworthings, and in a minor name, Ledewarden, suggesting again an influence from the Midlands not extending beyond the Ribble. The third form is the development of OE _æcer_, 'measure of land', in Cliviger, where _g_ represents the initial sound of _judge_; this development is seen only in Alsager in Cheshire among other place-names and may well be a Mercian form; minor names such as Goldacher and Wallecher show the same development.

The place-name evidence therefore suggests that the Ribble valley became a dividing line between Mercian and Northumbrian areas. Some Northumbrian forms are found south of the R. Ribble, suggesting an early colonisation of the whole county from Northumbria, whereas Mercian forms are not found north of the Ribble, suggesting the limits of Mercian conquest.

Scandinavian Settlement   In 793 the monastery of Lindisfarne was sacked by a raiding party of Scandinavians. This date is a convenient starting-point for the period of Scandinavian invasion of England which culminated in the conquest of a large part of eastern and northern England by a large Scandinavian army and the official recognition of this area as 'The Danelaw' by the Anglo-Saxon king of Wessex, Alfred, in 878. Despite later attacks, Alfred was able to contain the Scandinavians and, under his son, Edward, his daughter, Æthelflæd, and her Mercian husband, Ethelred, the Danelaw was re-conquered and England re-unified during the tenth century.

There is little direct evidence for Lancashire during this period. It has, on the one hand, been pointed out that York, the capital of the Danelaw, was in the hands of the Scandinavians by 866 and that, although southern Mercia was apparently quite strong in the early ninth century, in 893 the Scandinavians moved to Chester, from which they were expelled into Wales. The Scandinavians also settled in the Isle of Man and Anglesey, and in Ireland, where they founded Dublin; and Lancashire was therefore a natural link in a Scandinavian empire. On the other hand, it is by no means certain that Lancashire formed part of the Danelaw, and there is evidence to suggest that much Scandinavian settlement came not from the east but in a secondary and later wave from Ireland and the offshore islands. In 902 the Scandinavians were driven out of Dublin and there is an account relating to the period just after this event which tells how the Scandinavian king Ingimund and his followers, who had left Ireland and had tried unsuccessfully to gain land in Wales, were allowed to settle peacefully near Chester by Æthelflæd; the account also relates how the Scandinavians later became aggressive and attacked Chester, and ends by saying that other battles occurred later. It is also known that the Scandinavian kingdom of Galloway was founded in defiance of the Norwegian king Harald Fairhair by one of his chiefs, Ketill Flatnose, and that when Harald invaded from the west he found no-one on the Isle of Man because they had all fled to Scotland. This account may indicate an emigration not only to Scotland but also to the neighbouring areas of Cumberland and Lancashire. A twelfth-century account of the grant of Amounderness to the see of York by king Æthelstan (924-40) says that he gained the land from 'the pagans', which suggests a Scandinavian colony there in the tenth century.

The place-name evidence can add considerably to this sketchy historical account. The distribution of names with Scandinavian elements is significant. There are large numbers of these names in Lonsdale North of the Sands, stretching from the coast back into the hills and merging with the large body of ON settlement-names in the Lake District. Another large concentration is found between the rivers Lune and Ribble, most in the coastal and lowland area but an appreciable number in the upland region. The concentration of names continues south of the Ribble down the coast, among the sandhills and mossland, and the Scandinavian coastal-settlements continue across the R. Mersey into the Wirral in Cheshire. There is, however, little evidence of settlement on the higher land to the east, Brinscall and Anglezarke being the only major examples. There is a further small concentration of names near Manchester, around the Mersey-Irwell valley, with Oldham and Sholver in the hills to the east. This group of names also has its southerly extension into Cheshire, in names such as Cheadle Hulme, Knutsford and Holmes Chapel. The distribution of the names therefore suggests that the main settlement was from the west into

41

the less densely populated lowland areas of coast and mossland. To the north, this concentration is quite large, extends inland, and may indeed have been reinforced from existing settlements in Yorkshire and the northern counties. In the southern part of Lancashire, however, the western settlers did not penetrate in any numbers across the plain, and the higher plainland separates their settlements from the small outcrop of settlements from Yorkshire and the east in the Manchester area.

The Scandinavians who settled in north and east England were mainly Danes, with some Norwegians; those who settled later from the west, from primary settlements in Ireland and Man, were usually Norwegians, with some Celts. Although it is usually impossible to tell whether an ON name is Danish or Norwegian in origin, there are some 'test-words' which are frequently cited. Elements held to be distinctively Norwegian include *brekka*, 'hill', as in Breck; *búð*, as opposed to ODan. *bōth*, 'booth'; *erg*, 'shieling', a borrowing from Irish, as in Goosnargh; *gil*, 'ravine', added to a number of names; *skáli*, 'temporary hut', as in Scholes; and *slakki*, 'small shallow valley', as in Nettleslack. The elements held to be distinctively Danish include *hulm*, 'island, water-meadow', as opposed to the more general ON *holmr*, as in the Manchester group of Davyhulme, Hulme and Levenshulme; *porp*, 'secondary settlement', an element rare in Lancashire but seen in the minor name Gawthorpe; and, as noted above, *bōth*, 'booth', although this form is less conclusive than its Norwegian equivalent. It has been urged that the personal names which form the first elements of Urmston and Flixton, near Manchester, and of Hornby and Thirnby, on the R. Lune, are Danish.

The relative paucity of distinctively Danish elements and the relative frequency of distinctively Norwegian elements in Lancashire names would tend to confirm the view that Scandinavians in Lancashire were mostly Norwegians coming from the west. The occurrence of a number of distinctively Danish elements in the group of names around Manchester, however, suggests that there in particular we have the western limit of Danish settlement from the east.

Place-names can give some clues about the density and influence of the Scandinavian population. Names consisting only of ON elements, such as Crosby or Formby, suggest a strong and influential Scandinavian population locally, whereas names which contain an ON personal name in combination with an OE element, such as Urmston, suggest only the presence of Scandinavians in an Anglo-Saxon area. The coastal area in particular shows strong Scandinavian influence, and the hundreds of Amounderness and West Derby bear ON names. In the latter, the minor name Thingwall suggests an assembly for the purposes of law-making such as was usual in Scandinavian areas. But sure evidence of strong Scandinavian influence is provided by names which have preserved an ON inflection, indicating a knowledge of the grammatical system of ON among the population of the area, as in Windermere. In some cases elements occur in both ON and OE and it is difficult to say which has provided the basis of the modern name; but in general the evidence would seem to confirm the existence of a sizeable ON-speaking population in the western and northern areas of Lancashire from the tenth century, generally living in areas which were inhospitable and somewhat sparsely populated before that time.

French Influence   Very few Lancashire names are OF in origin — names such as Beaumont, Belmont and Bewsey are exceptions. In general OF influence results in the modification of certain names, in particular the substitution of *t* for *th* in names such as Tarbock and the substitution of *le* for *the* (originally some prepositional phrase such as *in the* or *by the*) as in Bolton-le-Sands or Poulton-le-Fylde. A number of other modifications in the representation of names in early records reflect OF spelling-conventions or pronunciations, but few have had any lasting influence.

5. Some Elements in Lancashire Place-Names

The purpose of this section is to present a few elements which are found frequently in Lancashire place-names and which can be used with a wide range of meanings. It is not convenient to discuss all the possible meanings on each occasion that the element occurs in a directory entry, nor is it always possible to be certain what the exact meaning is on each occasion. In many instances, therefore, the reader is referred to this section of the introduction. The discussion below is not concerned with the various problems of distribution, dialect and significance considered in the previous sections, but only with the range of forms and meanings which a few words may have.

The elements are listed in alphabetical order. In each entry, formal variations are discussed first, then the etymology and meanings. Each entry concludes with a list of all the names in the directory which contain the element. The basis for the entries is *EPNE*; the abbreviations used are those of the directory.

BURH, OE · Where it occurs as a first element, the word usually appears in the possessive form, *burge*, which develops as *bur-/ber-*. It is, however, more common as a second element, where it takes one of two forms:
  1 *burh*, nominative, which appears today as *-burgh/-borough*;
  2 *byrig*, dative, which appears today as *-bury*.
The element is the basis of modern *borough* and goes back to a Germanic root **burgs*, kin to the root of modern *borrow, bury*, with the sense 'protection, shelter'. *Burh* has the general sense of 'fortified place', but with a number of particular applications,

viz: 'earthwork, encampment', particularly of a prehistoric site, as in Arbury, 'the earth-*burh*'; 'Roman encampment, fort, station', as in Burrow; 'castle'; 'fortified house or manor', probably the usual sense in Lancashire names; and 'town', originally 'fortified town' but later 'market town', as in Flookburgh. The element is often combined with *tūn* (see below), as in Broughton-on-Irwell and Burtonwood, where the sense is 'enclosure round a fortified house'. Lancashire names containing the element include Arbury, Bilsborrow, Broughton-on-Irwell, Burrow, Burscough, Burtonwood, Bury, Didsbury, Duxbury, Flookburgh, Littleborough, Newburgh, Pendlebury, Salesbury, Samlesbury, Tilberthwaite.

BÝR, ON, BȲ, ODan. The ON form was *býr*; this develops as OWScand. *bær* and ODan. *bȳ*, but there is no certain evidence of the former in English names. The word has the same root as modern *bower*, *build*, Germanic **bū*, 'dwell, cultivate'. Before its introduction into England, it had a long history of use in Scandinavia where it seems to have had the senses of 'secondary settlement from an older existing settlement' and 'outlying farm'. In England, it means variously 'newly developed ground'; 'new or secondary settlement'; 'isolated farmstead'; and 'hamlet, village', probably the usual sense. The element was an obvious formal substitute for OE *burh/byrig* in sites re-named by Scandinavian settlers. Contrary to general Danelaw practice, few Lancashire names have the element in combination with a personal name. Lancashire names containing the element include Crosby, West Derby, Formby, Greetby, Hornby, Ireby, Kirkby, Nateby, Ribby, Roby, Sowerby, Subberthwaite, Westby.

HALH, OE   As a simplex, the word takes two forms — *haulgh*, from the nominative *halh*, and *hale* from the dative *hale*. As the first element of a name, it develops as *hal-*, as in Halsall and Halton, or *haugh-*, as in Haughton. As a final element it appears as either *-all*, as in Crumpsall and Hothersall, or perhaps *-halgh*, as in Ponthalgh. The *-all* ending has been confused with *hall* in Midge Hall. The word survives in dialectal *haugh* and is related to OE *holh*, modern *hollow*. It is usually translated as 'nook of land' when it appears in OE, but it develops a wide range of specific meanings in English place-names; viz. 'hollow in a hillside'; 'remote part of a parish'; 'land within the bend of a river' or 'tongue of land between two streams', as in Crumpsall; and 'piece of low-lying land by a river', the most frequent sense in Lancashire names Lancashire names containing the element include Catterall, Crumpsall, Ellel, Haighton, Hale, Halsall, Halton, Haughton, Haulgh, Hothersall, Kersal, Langho, Maghull, Midge Hall, Ordsall, Rossall, Ponthalgh, Westhoughton, Wolfhole Crag.

H̄AM, OE   Modern *home* derives from this word. From the Germanic base *xaim-* also derives the cognate ON word *heim,* 'home', which may be substituted for it in Scandinavian areas. It is readily confused with OE *hamm,* 'meadow' and may have influenced the written representation of some names with a dative pl. ending, -*um,* such as Lytham. It occurs almost invariably as a second or final element. Its meanings include 'house'; 'village'; 'manor'; 'religious household'. Lancashire names containing the element include Abram, Bispham, Cheetham, Cockerham, Heysham, Higham, Irlam, Kirkham, Penwortham, Rochdale (see directory), Tatham, Thornham. See also -*INGAHAM* below.

HOLMR, ON   The development of this form is to -*holme,* as opposed to ODan. *hulm* which develops to -*hulme.* The modern forms are a poor guide to origin since dialect developments of the two words are to an identical pronunciation and there is a tendency by French scribes to represent both by '-*o-*' forms. The word corresponds to an OE *holm,* 'sea', which, influenced by ON, later also comes to mean 'island'. It is generally supposed that the original meaning was 'hill' and that the word has the same origin as *hill.* It survives in dialect *holme,* used beyond the Danelaw by late ME. The ON sense is both 'islet' and 'meadow on a shore'. Although it can mean 'island', it usually has the sense in Lancashire names of 'higher ground in surrounding mossland or marsh' and more generally 'flat ground'. Lancashire names containing the element include Davyhulme, Dolphinholme, Dunnerholme, Eastham, Holme, Holmes, Hulme, Levenshulme, Oldham, Torrisholme.

HYRST, OE   The word comes from Germanic *hurst-* and has been held to be related to Welsh *prys,* 'brushwood'. The meaning seems to show a divergence from some base sense such as 'wooded eminence' since it means 'hillock', particularly of a sandy nature; 'sandbank'; 'copse'; 'wooded eminence'. Lancashire names containing the element include Ashurst, Collyhurst, Dewhurst, Gathurst, Hurst Green, Hurstwood, Limehurst, Nuthurst, Stonyhurst, Studlehurst.

-ING, -ING-, -INGAS, -INGAHĀM, -INGATŪN, OE   It is convenient to consider all these forms here since all depend for their meaning upon the interpretation of -*ing*. In many cases, modern names with -*ing*, such as Accrington or Haslingden, do not go back to a root in -*ing* at all but represent a later remodelling of some other form. The few that can be traced to an original -*ing* form present difficulties because this ending had a variety of uses — as a noun-forming suffix; as a place-name forming suffix; and as a patronymic form added to an OE personal name. An indication of an early place-name is the use of the group- or folk-name suffix -*ingas* (see section 4), but it is often impossible to establish the existence of the inflectional ending from the late evidence available for Lancashire names and difficult to distinguish the ending from the other suffixes already mentioned. The -*ingas* ending was quite distinct from the patronymic -*ing* and when combined with a personal name, it suggested probably some loose association of people depending on a common leader and living in a particular place rather than any blood relationship. This type of name suggests an early social structure, unlike a second use of the -*ingas* suffix, with a toponymic element, where the sense was rather 'the people living at or near' a particular place or physical feature; the topographical type of name remains productive throughout the Anglo-Saxon period, but its use with ending in -*ing* include:

1 popular remodelling — Dinckling
2 noun suffix — Chipping, Falinge, Newbigging
3 place-name suffix — Pilling, Wenning,
4 possible -*ingas* forms — Billinge, Bryning, Melling, Staining.

The possessive form of -*ingas, -inga*, in combination with a personal name, is found with other elements, particularly *lēah, hām, tūn, wīc. hām* is the ancestor of modern *home* and derives from Germanic **xaim-*; its usual sense in English names is 'village', but its meanings range from 'house' to 'manor, estate'. It remains productive throughout the Anglo-Saxon period, but its use with folk-names is limited to an early period of settlement. Lancashire names in -*ingham* include:

1 popular remodelling — Gressingham
2 -*ingahām* forms — Aldingham, Habergham, Padiham, Whittingham

Modern -*ington* forms which go back to an original -*ing* suffix added to an OE personal name may represent one of two possibilities. The first is the possessive form of *ingas, -inga*, as in the *ingaham* forms above; the second is a connective particle

-ing-, uninflected, linking the first element — personal name or ordinary word — to the second. The meaning of this connective particle seems to be rather vague but may be summed up as '*tūn* which pertains to' someone or something. The usage is not datable to an early period. Again, the evidence for the inflectional *-a-* of a true *-ingatūn* form has usually disappeared by the time a Lancashire name is first recorded. Lancashire names in *-ington* include:

1 popular remodelling — Accrington, Farington, Paddington (coined name), Shevington, Whittington, Withington, Wrightington
2 with first elements ending in *-ing* — Pennington, Rivington, Wennington
3 with word and *-ingtūn* — Dumplington, Warrington,
4 with personal name and *-ington* (either *-ingtūn* or *-ingatūn*) — Addington, Adlington, Alkrington, Billington (?), Pilkington, Pleasington, Tottington, Worthington

On the meaning of *tūn,* see below.

LĒAH, OE The element derives from an Indo-European root **louq—* which is related to the root of the modern noun *light* and is also the basis of Latin *lūcus*, 'grove' It survives as modern *lea*. The word seems to have referred both to 'woodland' and to 'a clearing in a wood', probably its usual sense in place-names. The clearing may simply have been 'a woodland glade', but the element often refers also to 'a cultivated clearing in woodland used for pastoral or arable farming'. At a later stage of its development, the word develops the meaning of 'open land, meadow-land', a sense aided by the possible formal confusion of the plural, *lēas*, with OE *lǣs*, 'pasture, meadow-land'. The element, most common in wooded areas, occurs only in final position where it usually develops the modern form *-ly, -ley*. Lancashire names containing the element include Appley Bridge, Arley, Arpley, Ashley, Astley, Bailey, Bardsley, Barley, Beesley, Birchley, Blackley, Buckley, Burnley, Cadley, Chaigley, Chorley, Cleveley Bank, Cuerdley, Dearnley, Dinckley, Dineley, Fazakerley, Greystoneley, Healey, Hindley, Kearsley, Kingsley, Knowley, Knowsley, Langley, Lea Town, Leigh, Luzley, Mawdesley, Mearley, Mossley, Osmotherley, Prestolee, Reedley, Risley, Roughlee Booth, Royley, Shakerley, Staveley, Thornley, Towneley, Tunley, Tyldesley, Walmersley, Westleigh, Whalley, Wheatley, Whelley, Winmarleigh, Winstanley, Worsley.

TŪN, OE   The commonest element in English place-names and source of modern *town*, the word derives from a CGerm. **tūnaz, *tūnam*, 'fence, hedge', which also appears in ON *tún*. The word develops a range of meanings in OE, viz. 'enclosed piece of ground'; 'building with its enclosed piece of ground, farmstead'; 'hamlet, village'; 'manor, estate'. The modern sense of 'conurbation larger than a village with a greater degree of administrative independence' is found in ME and is usually too late to influence place-names; in the majority of cases, 'farm' or 'village' is the probable meaning. Although usually a final element, it can appear as a first element, notably in the compounds **tūn-stall*, 'site of a farm', as in Tunstall and Rawtenstall; and *tūn-stede*, 'farm-stead', found in the minor name Tunstead. Lancashire names containing *tūn* include Accrington, Aighton, Alkrington, Allerton, Alston, Anderton, Angerton, Appleton, Ashton, Atherton, Aughton, Balderstone, Barton, Bolton, Bretherton, Broughton, Burtonwood, Carleton, Castleton, Caton, Chadderton, Chatterton, Chorlton, Churchtown, Claughton, Clayton, Clifton, Colton, Coniston, Crompton, Cronton, Croston, Dalton, Denton, Ditton, Dumplington, Dutton, Eccleston, Edenfield, Egton, Elston, Elton, Eltonhead, Euxton, Everton, Farington, Farleton, Flixton, Forton, Freckleton, Gleaston, Gorton, Gressingham, Haighton, Halton, Hambleton, Hapton, Haughton, Heaton, Hilderstone, Hoghton, Houghton Green, Hurlston, Hutton, Huyton, Layton, Little Hulton, Little Mitton, Longton, Lowton, Martin Mere, Marton, Middleton, Monton, Moston, Netherton, Newton, Osbaldeston, Overton, Paddington (coined name), Pendleton, Pennington, Pilkington, Pleasington, Plumpton, Poulton, Preston, Priest Hutton, Ribbleton, Rishton, Rivington, Rixton, Royton, Scorton, Sefton, Shevington, Singleton, Skerton, Stainton, Sutton, Swinton, Tarleton, Taunton, Thistelton, Thornton, Towneley, Tunley, Tunstall, Turton, Twiston, Ulverston, Upton, Urmston, Walton, Warrington, Warton, Weeton, Wennington, Westhoughton, Wheelton, Whittington, Winton, Withington, Witton, Woodplumpton, Woolston, Woolton, Worston, Worthington, Wrayton, Wrightington.

WĪC, OE   The usual form of the word in Lancashire names is *-wick*, from the nominative *wīc*, but the *-wich* ending of Prestwich is from an oblique case such as the dative. The word was borrowed in Germanic from Latin *vīcus*, 'row of houses, street, city district'. It seems to have had the sense of 'dwelling' or, in the plural (which is formally identical to the singular in the nominative), 'a collection of dwellings'. It is used as 'building for a particular occupation or purpose', as in Borwick and Fishwick, and in particular 'farm', especially 'dairy farm'. Lancashire names containing the element include Ardwick, Beswick, Borwick, Chadwick, Elswick, Fishwick, Prestwich, Salwick, Urswick, Winwick, Wycoller.

FURTHER READING

Studies of Lancashire Place-names

Ekwall, E., *The Place-Names of Lancashire,* Chetham Society, Manchester, 1922.

Harrison, H., *The Place-Names of the Liverpool District,* Elliot Stack, London, 1898.

Potter, S., 'South-West Lancashire Place-Names', *Transactions of the Historic Society of Lancashire and Cheshire,* vol. 111, 1960, pp. 1-24.

Sephton, J., *A Handbook of Lancashire Place-Names,* Henry Young and Sons, Liverpool, 1913.

Wyld, H.C., and Hirst, T.O., *The Place-Names of Lancashire: Their Origin and History,* Constable, London, 1911.

Reference Works

Ekwall, E., *English River-Names,* Clarendon Press, Oxford, 1928.

Ekwall, E., *The Concise Oxford Dictionary of English Place-Names,* 4th. edition, Clarendon Press, Oxford, 1960.

Nicolaisen, M.F., Gelling, M., and Richards, M., *The Names of Towns and Cities in Britain,* Batsford, 1970.

Smith, A.H., *English Place-Name Elements,* English Place-Name Society vols. 25 and 26, Cambridge University Press, 1956.

Other Works

Ashmore, O., *The Industrial Archaeology of Lancashire,* David and Charles, Newton Abbot, 1969.

Bagley, J.J., *A History of Lancashire with Maps and Pictures,* Darwen Finlayson Ltd., Beaconsfield, 1967.

Cameron, K., *English Place Names,* Batsford, third edition, 1977.

Collins, H.C., *Lancashire: Plain and Seaboard,* J.M. Dent and Sons Ltd., London, 1953.

Fleetwood Hesketh, P., *Murray's Lancashire Architectural Guide,* John Murray, 1955.

Gelling, Margaret, *Signposts to the Past: Place-names and the History of England*, J.M. Dent and Sons Ltd., London 1978.

Gelling, Margaret, *Place-names in the Landscape*, J.M. Dent and Sons Ltd., London, 1984.

Millward, R., *Lancashire: An Illustrated Essay on the History of the Landscape*, Hodder and Stoughton, London, 1955.

Shaw, R.C., *The Royal Forest of Lancaster*, The Guardian Press, Preston. 1956.

Wainwright, F.T., *Archaeology and Place-Names and History: An Essay on Problems of Co-ordination*, Routledge and Kegan Paul, 1962.

Maps

Saxton's Map of Lancashire, 1577, British Museum Maps C.7.c.1, 1961.

William Yates's Map of Lancashire, 1786, ed. by J.B. Harley, The Historic Society of Lancashire and Cheshire, 1968.

Reprint of the first edition of the one-inch Ordnance Survey of England and Wales, sheets 15, 16, 19, 20, 21, 26, 27, David and Charles, Newton Abbot, 1970.

The above list is limited mainly to recent and readily available works. It may be supplemented by the references in the *Preface* and from the publications of the Historic Society of Lancashire and Cheshire, of the Lancashire and Cheshire Antiquarian Society, of the Chetham Society and of the Record Society of Lancashire and Cheshire. Many towns have useful local guides which include some account of the origins of the minor names of the area. The Victoria History of the county is an essential research tool, and the publications of the English Place-Name Society provide important evidence for other counties.

Anyone wishing to undertake original work on Lancashire place-names may well find manuscript material in his local reference library, or in the library of an institution such as the University of Liverpool, the University of Manchester or Stonyhurst College. The most important collection of material is in the County Record Office, Preston. Useful material may be found, as Lenney has demonstrated, in the Diocesan Registry, Lichfield. Other material may be found in the British Museum, the Public Record Office and the various city record offices.

Note

For a list of abbreviations used, see p.9.
The following conventions are observed:
1. Cross-reference
   To another directory entry – *KENYON*
   To an entry on the list of elements in section 5 – OE *halh.*
2. Where an entry has a Latinised ending which may confuse the reader, (Latin) is placed at the end of the reference.
3. Where an element not of OE origin has been given the OE possessive inflection -es, the inflection has not been indicated to be of OE origin.
4. Relationship
   Of one word in the etymology to another – +
   Of one form in the name's development to another – →

A

Abbeystead the site of the abbey (OF ab(b)eie + OE stede). The name is believed to indicate the site of the Cistercian abbey of Wyresdale, an offshoot of Furness Abbey, which was founded at the end of the twelfth century but closed before 1204 when the monks moved to Wotheney in Ireland. The earliest recorded reference to the place is vaccary del Abbey (1323), 'the dairy farm of the abbey'. However, Abbeystead also occurs as a minor name, referring to three fields in Upper Rawcliffe, in a bend in the R. Wyre, and it has been suggested that this would be a more probable site for the abbey than that in the royal forest of Wyresdale suggested by the major name. If so, the meaning might rather be 'estate owned by the abbey', as in the earliest reference. On stede in the sense of 'site of a religious house', compare *STIDD*.

Abbey Village The village consists of workers' cottages built beside the former Abbey Mill, a cotton mill of c.1840. The Abbey of Stanlow, later transferred to Whalley, held land in the township of Withnell within which the village stands.

Abram Eadburh's *hām* (OE Eadburh + hām → Adburgham 1199 → Abburgham 1246 → Abraham 1372 → Abram 1461). Eadburh was a woman's name.

Accrington *tūn* where acorns are found (OE æcern + tūn → Akarinton pre-1194 → Acrinton 1277 → Akeringtone 1296 → Ackryngton 1311). The town's location on the edge of the forest of Rossendale, and the importance of acorns as food for pigs, make the above etymology probable, but this would be the only example of an English major name containing æcern. The vill of Accrington was depopulated in the Middle Ages by the monks of Kirkstall Abbey in order to create a grange for the abbey.

Addington *tūn* associated with Eadda (OE Eadda + -ingtūn → Addington 1786). The hamlet stands in high land north of the R. Lune and several early settlement names are found in the Lune valley. The name may be of the -ingatūn type (see Introduction, p. 46), but it is recorded very late and much earlier forms would be needed to establish a definite etymology and confirm it as possible evidence of early Anglo-Saxon settlement.

Adgarley Edgar's slope (OE Eadgār + hliᵭ → Eadgarlith 1185 → Adgerlith c.1300), referring to the situation of the place. The hamlet is now joined with *STAINTON*.

Adlington *tūn* associated with Eadwulf (OE Ēadwulf + *-ingtūn* → Edeluinton 1190 → Adelventon 1202 → Adelinton 1246 → Adlington 1288). The name may be indicative of early Anglo-Saxon settlement, but earlier forms are needed to establish this fact.

Aigburth oak-tree hill (ON eik + berg → Aykeberh c.1200 → Aykeberue pre-1247 → Ayberc c.1242). The suburb is on a ridge and includes Mossley Hill.

Aighton oak-tree *tūn* (OE āc + tūn → Actun DB → Aiton 1102 → Aghton c.1140). For a different development, compare *AUGHTON*.

Ainsdale Ægenwulf's valley (OE Ægenwulf + -es (possessive) + dæl → Einulvesdeᵢ DB → Ainuluesdal c.1192 → Aynolfsdale 1336 → Aynolsdale 1451). The form of the name is OE, but it may well also have been influenced by the ON personal name Einulfr and by ON dalr, 'valley', as the DB form may indicate; there is a concentration of ON names in this coastal area. The site, between sandhills and mossland, suggests the sense of low-lying land.

Ainsworth Ægen's enclosure (OE Ægen + -es (possessive) + worᵭ → Haineswrthe c.1200 → Ainesworth 1244). The first part is a shortened form of some OE compound-name, such as Ægenbald or Ægenwulf.

Aintree a single tree (ON einn + tré → Ayntre 1220). A single tree would be conspicuous in this flat landscape and could serve to mark a boundary or a meeting-place.

Aldcliffe the high land long occupied (OE ald + clif → Aldeclif DB). The reference is to the high land east of the R. Lune on which the village stands. Used with topographical features, ald may mean 'long used' or 'formerly used'. It has been suggested that the first element may be the OE personal name Alda; this is possible, but clif is rarely found in combination with personal names.

Aldingham *hām* of Alda's people (OE Ald(a) + ingahām → Aldingham DB). The name is indicative of early Anglo-Saxon settlement (see introduction, pp.46).

Alkincoats Etymology doubtful (Altenecote 1201 → Alcancotes 1296). The second element would seem to be OE cot, 'cottage'.

Alkrington Hall *tūn* associated with Alhhere (OE Alhher(e) + ingtūn → Alkinton 1212 → Alkrington 1311). This minor name is frequently cited as an *-ingatūn* form, possibly indicative of early Anglo-Saxon settlement, although earlier forms are needed to establish this fact (see introduction, pp. 46).

Allerton alder *tūn* (OE alor + tūn → Alretune DB → Allerton 1292).

Allithwaite Eilif's clearing (ON Eil-ífr + þveit → Hailiuethait c.1175 → Aliuthwait c.1210 → Alithwait 1327), the name of a village and the parishes of LOWER and UPPER ALLITHWAITE.

Alston Ælf's *tūn* (OE Ælf + -es (possessive) + tūn → Alston 1226 → Halleston 1246 → Alfston c.1250). Ælf is a shortened form of some OE compound-name such as Ælfsige.

Alt The name of a river and a village, with different etymologies:
(1) river, flowing through low-lying ground in south-west Lancashire: 'marsh' (Celt. *alet → Alt c.1190);
(2) village among hills south-west of Oldham: 'hill' (Welsh allt → Alt c.1200).

Altcar marshy land beside the R. *ALT* (ALT + ON kjarr → Acrer DB → Altekar 1251).

Altham water-meadow where swans are found (OE ælfitu + hamm → Elvetham c.1150 → Alvetham 1243 → Altham 1383). The village is near the R. Calder.

Amounderness Agmund's headland (ON Agmund(r) + -ar (possessive) + nes → Agemvndrenesse DB → Amondernesia 1094 (Latin) → Hamundernes c.1190 → Aumundernesse 1242). The headland bears the name of a Scandinavian who must have held considerable authority; it has been suggested that he was the Agmund who was killed at the battle of Tettenhall in 910 and who is known to have belonged to north-ern England, but this cannot be proved. VCH notes that 'Hagemund occurs locally as a personal name'.

It is not clear to which headland the name refers, although Rossall Point has been suggested. At the time of the Conquest it was already a district name and later became the name of one of the six hundreds of Lanca-shire. Some later forms, such as Andreness 1535, suggest a continu-ing modification of the name and Camden confirms that in his time it was locally called Anderness, but this tendency seems to have been reversed later.

Ancoats the lonely cottage (OE ān + cot → Einecote 1212 → Hanekotes 1243 → Ancoates c.1250). The earl-iest recorded form shows influence from ON einn, 'one, lonely'.

Anderton Eanred's *tūn* (OE Ēanrēd + tūn → Anderton 1212).

Anfield ? the field on a slope (ME hange + OE feld → Hongfield 1642 → Annfield 1786), probably a minor name of late origin.

Angerton *tūn* by a bay (ON angr + OE tūn → Angertona 1293 (Latin) → Angerton 1299). The hamlet is on the estuary of the R. Duddon, to which the name may refer. The hamlet is in mossland, with Angerton Marsh (mariscum de Angertuna c.1300) to the south. OE *anger, 'grassland, pasture land', has also been proposed for the first element of the name; the minor names of Herd House and Herd House Moss occur nearby.

Anglezarke hill-pasture belonging to Anlaf (OE Anlaf + -es (possessive) + ON erg → Andelevesarewe 1202 → Anlauesargh 1224 → Anleshargh c.1240). Anlaf is from an early form

55

of the ON personal name Oláfr.

Angram (at) the pasture lands (OE *anger, in the form *angrum (dative pl.) → Angrum 1332).

Ansdell The suburb of Lytham was named after the painter Richard Ansdell who lived there.

Appleton apple *tūn,* i.e. orchard (OE æppel + tūn → Apelton 1182).

Appletreeworth The absence of early forms makes etymology doubtful, but the name would appear to mean 'enclosure where appletrees grow'.

Appley Bridge apple-tree clearing (OE æppel + lēah → Appelae 13th.c. → Appley 13th.c.). The hamlet is at a bridging-point of the R. Douglas and of the Leeds-Liverpool Canal.

Arbury earth *burh* (OE eorþ + burh, in the form byrig (dative) → Herdbiri c.1215 → Herbury 1243 → Erthbury 1246 → Erbury 1332). The reference may be to a prehistoric earthwork, now lost.

Ardwick Æthelred's *wīc* (OE Æðelrēd + -es (possessive) + wīc → Atheriswyke 1282 → Ardewike 1322). It is not usual to find a personal name combined with wīc.

Arkholme (at) the hill-pastures (ON erg + -um (dative pl.) → Ergune DB → Argun 1195 → Argham 1501 → Arckholme 1662). The form of the name has been modified through the confusion of the ending with ON *holmr*, dial. holme, 'higher dry ground among marshes'; this confusion may have been aided both by the situation of the village on

higher land by the R. Lune and also by the existence of the major name *HOLME* to the north-west.

Arnside Arni's mountain pasture (ON Arni + sǽtr → Arnolvesheved 1246 → Ernesyde 1537). See also *HAWES WATER.*

Ashhurst Beacon ash-tree hill (OE æsc + hyrst → Aschehyrst 1285 → Asshurst c.1310). *Hyrst* clearly has the sense of 'wooded eminence' here. The 570-foot hill was clearly a place where a beacon-fire was made for signalling purposes, hence the addition of OE bēacon, 'beacon', in the modern period; the present beacon was re-erected c1800 in anticipation of French invasion.

Ashley ash-tree *lēah* (OE æsc + lēah → Esseleye 1220 → Asheleigh 1323).

Ashton ash-tree *tūn* (OE æsc + tūn), the name of four places:
(1) north of Out Rawcliffe (By Asshton 1332);
(2) on the R. Lune, south of Lancaster (Estun DB → Astuna c.1155 (Latin) → Aschton 1226). The earliest form, which recurs throughout the 13th-15th. centuries, probably shows the substitution of ON eski, 'place growing with ash-trees', for OE æsc. The parish name is ASHTON WITH *STODDAY;*
(3) ASHTON IN *MAKERFIELD* (Eston 1212 → Ayston 1246 → Ashton 1255) — on the earliest form, see (2) above;
(4) ASHTON UNDER *LYNE* (Haistune c1160 → Eston 1212 → Asheton 1276).
The defining additions in (3) and (4) are required because the name

is so frequent.

Askam-in-Furness (at) the ash-trees (ON ask(r) + -um (dative pl) → ?Askeham 1535). The earliest form is doubtful and late. The etymology here proposed is that also for Askham (We), from which the defining addition distinguishes the Lancashire town, but it is possible that some word such as OE hām or hamm, or ON holmr, rather than an inflectional ending, constitutes the second element.

Asland (R) ash-tree river (ON askr + OE lane → Asklone 1217 → Ascalon 1223 → Asteland 1550 → Astland c.1555 → the River Douglas alias Asland 1719). Lane here has the sense of dial. lane, 'the course of a stream in meadowland'; the name refers to the lower reaches of the R. DOUGLAS below Tarleton, where it flows through low-lying land.

Aspull aspen hill (OE æspe + hyll → Aspul 1212 → Apshull 1246). The town stands on a ridge of high land and the parish today has been called 'a treeless tract'.

Astley the east lēah (OE ēast + lēah → Astelege c.1210 → Asteleye 1304). The name may have been given in distinction to LEIGH, to the west. As with LEIGH, the situation of the hamlet, in mossland, makes the sense of 'meadow land' probable for lēah.

Atherton Æthelhere's tūn (OE Æðelhere + tūn → Aderton 1212 → Atherton 1322).

Audenshaw Aldwine's copse (OE Aldwine + sceaga → Aldenesawe c.1200 → Aldenshagh c.1250).Sceaga is rarely found with a personal name.

Aughton oak-tree tūn (OE āc + tūn), the name of two villages:
(1) near Ormskirk (Achetun DB → Acton 1235 → Aghton 1282 → Aughton 1311);
(2) near the R. Lune (Acheton 1212 → Acton 1246 → Aghton 1326 → Aughton 1650).
Despite the similarity of forms, (1) is pronounced 'Orton' and (2) 'Afton'. For a different development, compare AIGHTON.

Aynesome Manor (at) the lonely houses (OE ān + hūs + -um (dative pl.) → Aynson 1491).

Ayre gravel bank (ON eyrr), a common element in names of the Lune valley referring to islands, low land by the river, former sandbanks, etc. Green Ayre (Eyre 1271) is now part of Lancaster; other minor names include Salt Ayre, High Ayre and Low Ayre.

Ayside etymology doubtful (Aysshed 1491 → Aysyde 1591). The first element appears to be ON á, 'river', but forms are too late to determine the second element — both OE hēafod, 'headland', and ON sǽtr, 'summer pasture', have been suggested. The form has at least been influenced by OE sīde, 'land extending alongside a river'. The name is that of a hamlet and also of a river, Ayside Pool, a tributary of the R. EEA. Possibly both river and tributary were once called á, but the latter was later given a distinctive name.

B

Backbarrow hill with a ridged or back-like top (OE bæc + beorg → Bakbarowe 1537). The village is in hilly country on the R. Leven.

Bacup valley by a ridge (OE bæc + hop → Fulebachope c.1200 → Bacop 1324). Hop has the specific sense of 'small enclosed valley, esp. one overlooking the main valley'; Bacup stands on the R. Irwell, in a valley off the main river valley, with higher ground to the west. This sense of hop is first recorded in ME and ON influence on the sense development has been suggested. The earliest recorded form has as its first element OE fūl, 'foul, dirty', which is usually found only with water terms, while the form of the second element suggests OE bæce, ME (WMidl) bache, 'stream, valley', perhaps suggesting some confusion of, or an alternative, etymology.

Bagslate Moor ? badger's valley (OE *bagga + slæd → Bagslade 13th. c.) The first element is attested only in place-names, where its use suggests that it referred to some 'bag-like' animal; the badger would seem the most appropriate English reference. OE mōr, 'moor', is a later addition.

Bailey lēah where berries grow (OE beg + lēah → Baillee 1204).

Balderstone Baldhere's tūn (OE Baldhere + -s (possessive) + tūn), the name of two places:
(1) on the R. Ribble, sometimes listed as BALDERSTON (Balderestone, Balderston, Baldeston 1246);
(2) south of Rochdale (Baldreston 1323). In both cases there has been confusion with OE stān, 'stone', at some stage in the name's development.

Bamber Bridge etymology doubtful (Bymbrig, undated). It has been suggested that the name means 'Bimme's bridge' (OE Bimme + brycg), but brycg is only rarely associated with persons and there are insufficient early forms. The bridge was over the R. Lostock and was formerly maintained jointly by the hundreds of Blackburn and Leyland.

Bamford ford where there is a beam (OE bēam + ford → Bamford 1228). The name probably implies that there was a footbridge by the ford. Bamford Hall is near the R. Roch and a tributary.

Bamfurlong strip of land where beans are grown (OE b ēan + furlang → Banforthlang 1442→ Banforlonge 1553 → Bamferlonge 1584). Beans were an important food and b ēan is an element also found in Lancashire minor names.

Bank Quay river bank (OE banca → Bank Fyelds 1587 → Bank Key 1712). The name originally referred to fields by the R. Mersey, which in the seventeenth century became the site of Thomas Patten's copper works. Patten claimed to have made the Mersey navigable from Liverpool to Warrington in order to ship ore to his works, hence the change of name recorded in the early eighteenth century.

Banks bank (The Bank 1713), referring to higher land between Martin Mere and the sea. It is possible that the sense of 'bank of earth to restrain water' is implied by the name.

Barbers Moor etymology doubtful (Barblismor c.1200 → Barbars more 1639). The earliest form still survives in an alternative name Barbles Moor.

Bardsea Beorda's 'island' (OE Beornrǣd + -es (possessive) + ēg → Berretseige DB → Berdeseia 1155 (Latin). Beorda is a shortened form of Beornrǣd. The second element refers to the raised site overlooking Morecambe Bay on which the village stands.

Bardsley Beord's *lēah* (OE Beornrǣd + -es (possessive) + lēah → Bar-

desley 1422). Beord is a shortened form of Beornrǣd.

Bare grove (OE bearu → Bare DB).

Barker etymology doubtful (Barker 1513). The earliest recorded form is too late for certainty, although ME *barkarie, 'sheep-fold', is a possibility.

Barley (Bayrlegh 1324). Two etymologies have been proposed – 'glade where boars are found or kept' (OE b ār + lēah); and 'clearing where barley is grown' (OE bere + lēah). If the latter etymology is preferred, the first element would be a by-form of OE bere, bær or ON barr, 'barley' and the name would be relatively late, referring to the clearance of the forest-area; since the area was predominantly a dairy-farming region, the cultivation of grain might well be distinctive. Compare *WHEATLEY*.

Barnacre barley-field (OE beren + æcer → Berneacre 1517). The name appears in the parish-name BARNACRE WITH *BONDS*.

Barnside Biǫrn's mountain pasture (ON Biǫrn + sǽtr → Bernesete 1258 → Bernesyde 1508 → Barneside 1535). In the later development of the name, the second element has been replaced by OE sīde, 'the long slope of a hill', which suits the hillside situation.

Barrow The name of several places in the county, major and minor, with two different etymologies:
(1) grove (OE bear(u) + -we (dative sg.), as in BARROW near Clitheroe (Barowclough 1324); BAR-

ROW NOOK (Barwe 1332); BAR-ROW HALL near Prescot, a minor name (Barwe 1284);

(2) For BARROW-IN-*FURNESS* the etymology is different. The name was originally that of an island (Barrai 1190), later called Old Barrow (Oldebarrey 1537, Old Barro Insula, Barrohead 1577) and joined to the mainland; the town took the name of the island. The name seems to mean 'island with promontory' (Brit. *barro- + ON ey), but it is probable that the Scandinavian settlers accepted *barro- as a meaningless name to which they added an explanatory ON second element.

Barrowford the ford by a grove (OE bearu + ford → Barouforde 1296). The village stands on the west bank of the Pendle Water and is distinguished from the nearby hamlets of Higherford and Lowerford.

Bartle tongue of land on which barley grows (OE bere + tægl → Bartayl 1256). The hamlets of HIGHER and LOWER BARTLE are on slightly higher ground which, to the east, separates the Woodplumpton and Sharoe Brooks. The possibility that the first element is OE bār, 'boar', cannot be completely discounted in a wooded area such as this was.

Barton barley *tūn* (OE bere + tūn), the name of three places:
(1) north of Preston (Bartun DB);
(2) near Altcar (Bartune DB);
(3) BARTON - UPON - *IRWELL* (Barton 1196).
The first element is a by-form of OE bere, bær, perhaps influenced

by ON barr, 'barley'. Compare *PEMBERTON*.

Baxenden the valley where baking-stones are found (OE *bæc-stān + denu → Bastanedenecloch 1194 → Bakestandene 1305 → Baxtonden 1464). The earliest form includes OE *clōh, 'ravine'.

Baycliffe the cliff where beacon-fires are lit (OE bēl + clif → Bellecliue 1212 → Beacliff 1585). The hamlet is on a cliff by the coast. It is possible that the name may refer to a cremation rather than a beacon fire. Some confusion has arisen with OF bel, beau, 'fair, beautiful'.

Bay Horse The place takes its name from the Old Bay Horse Inn. The name gained currency when adopted as that of the railway station, closed in 1960.

Bazil Point etymology doubtful (Basul c.1200). It has been suggested that the name consists of a personal name combined with OE hyll, 'hill'.

Beal (R) the winding stream (OE bēogol → Bole c.1220 → Bele c.1300). The name is also seen in BEAL MOOR (Belemore 1323).

Beardwood Bearda's enclosure (OE Bearda + worð → Berdewrthe 1258 → Berdworthe 1296 → Berdwood 1609). At a late stage in the development of the name, worð has been replaced by OE wudu, 'wood'.

Beaumont beautiful hill (OF beau + mont → Belli Montis 1190 → Belmunt 1212 → Beaumont 13th c.). The form is evidenced in a number of minor names north of Lancaster. It is one of the few names of OF origin and, although it suits the high situation of BEAUMONT GRANGE, it may well have been adopted because it was common in France. Compare nearby BELMOUNT.

Becconsall Bekan's hill (ON Bekan + -es (possessive) + haugr → Bekaneshou 1208). The personal name is Irish in origin, adopted by the Norwegian settlers during their period in Ireland. The name seems to refer to a ridge which falls to low land by the R. Ribble. Although it has been argued from this situation that the first element could be OE bēacon, 'beacon', referring to a beacon used to guide travellers crossing the river by the sands route, this etymology is improbable; OE bēacon is not common in names before the fifteenth century.

Bedford Beda's ford (OE Bēda + ford → Bedeford 1201), referring presumably to a ford over the Pennington Brook.

Beesley ? lēah where bent grass grows (OE *bēos + lēah → Beselaye c.1200). Derivation from ON Bisi, a personal name, has also been proposed.

Belfield open country by the R. BEAL (BEAL + OE feld → Belefeld 1310).

Belmount beautiful hill (OE bel + mont → Belmunt 1212). Since beau, rather than bel, would be expected here, as in nearby BEAUMONT, OE bēl, 'fire, funeral pyre', and OE belle, 'bell, i.e. bell-shaped' have

been proposed as alternatives for the first element. However, since there is evidence of OF influence in the area and since the second element is OF, the etymology proposed here seems preferable. Strict grammatical agreement may not have been observed at the time of the name's formation, and it provides a convenient distinction from nearby *BEAUMONT.*

Bescar marshy ground where birch trees grow (OE birce + ON kjarr → Birchecar 1331). The earliest recorded form is late and the possibility of an original ON first element, birki, 'birch-wood', cannot be excluded. The first element has undergone considerable modification, which may include confusion with OE beorc, 'birch-tree'.

Beswick ? Bēac's wīc (OE Bēac + -es (possessive) + wīc → Bexwic c.1210). Earlier forms are needed for a more certain etymology.

Bethecar etymology doubtful (Bothaker 1509 → Bethokar c.1538 → Betaker 1537). Earlier forms are needed.

Bewsey beautiful site (OF beau + sé → Beausee 1330 → Bewsey 1503). The housing estate is named from BEWSEY HALL; the original hall was built by William le Boteler on land bought in c.1264 from the monks of Tiltey Abbey in Essex who had a grange there called beau site.

Bickershaw beekeepers' copse (OE bīcere + sceaga → Bikersah c.1200 → Bykershagh 1395).

Bickerstaffe ? river bank belonging to beekeepers (OE bīcere + stæð → Bikerstad 1190 → Bikerstath 1226 → Bikerstaff 1267). The name presents a number of problems. BICKERSTAFFE is in flat country, some former mossland with small woods and streams. The sense of 'river bank' or the later sense of stæð, 'landing place', is not obviously appropriate; moreover, the ON cognate stǫð, 'landing place', would also be possible. The earliest form shows possible influence from OE stede, 'place', and later forms may reflect its cognate, ON staðr, 'place, site'; this latter element is rare in England, partly because it is indistinguishable from stæð and stǫð which usually give adequate sense, but it might be preferable here. The second element has undergone further changes on analogy to the familiar OE stæf, 'staff', although forms in -stath are well attested. Attempts to relate the first element to OE bece, 'beech-tree', are unconvincing.

Bigforth ? clearing where barley grows (ON bygg + þveit → Biggetheit 1242 → Bigthvait 1246). Ekwall notes that the identity of early forms with the place is not certain. If they do refer to BIGFORTH, þveit has later been replaced with the NCy development of OE ford, 'ford'. There is no stream at this place, but the change could have been influenced by the nearby name of *SCOTFORTH* and perhaps by association of the first element with 'big'.

Biggar a triangular piece of land where barley grows (ON bygg + geiri → Bigger 1292).

Billinge hill (OE bill + -ing- + -e (locative)), the name of two hills: (1) near Witton (Billingehill 1429); (2) near Wigan, where it is also the name of the nearby village (Billing 1202 → Bulling c.1200 → Billyngge 1332).
It has been suggested that the name derives from OE bill, 'sword, edge; hence prominent hill', to which has been added the suffix -ing with the old locative inflexion. The sense would suit both sites – the 807-foot hill near Witton and the 589-foot hill above the Lancashire plain near Wigan. However, derivation from an OE personal name, Billa, has also been proposed and the name has been cited as an example of the -ingas name-type characteristic of early settlement (see introduction pp. 46-7); the sense would then be 'people associated with Billa' and the name would be a folk-name; see also *BILLINGTON*.

Billington (Billingduna 1196 (Latin) → Billingdon 1203 → Billinton 1208). The name refers to a long ridge to the south-east of the present settlement, now called BILLINGTON MOOR (Billingahoth c.1130). Early forms above show that the name is a combination of BILLING and OE dūn, 'hill', and that the final element has later been confused with OE tūn, aided no doubt by the transfer of the name to the settlement beneath the ridge. The c.1130 form has OE hōh, 'spur', as final element. BILLING presents the same problem as *BILLINGE*, being either a hill-name itself (OE bill + -ing) or a folk-name (OE Bill(a) + -ing- + a (possessive pl)). By the former etymology, the ridge would originally have been called

BILLING(E) and an explanatory final element would have been added later, the whole being transferred to the settlement at an even later stage. By the latter etymology, the first part of the name would refer to a group of people and their leader associated with the ridge. It has been pointed out that BILLINGE HILL, BILLINGE SCAR, BILLING-TON and BILLINGTON MOOR are all on higher ground south of the R. Ribble and mark out a possible folk-territory approximately seven miles long.

Bilsborrow Bill's *burh* (OE Bill + -es (possessive) + burh → Billesbure 1187 → Billesburgh 1212 → Bilsborough 1508 → Bilsburrow 1632).

Birch birch-tree (OE birce → Birches 1246).

Birchley birch-tree *lēah* (OE birce + lēah → Biricherelee 1202 → Birchley 1422).

Birkacre field by a birch-copse (ON birki + akr → Birkaker c.1240).

Birkdale birch-tree valley (ON birki + dalr → Birkedale c.1200). BIRK-DALE is the surviving portion of Argarmeols (ON Erengr + melr → Erengermeles DB), 'Erengr's sand-hill', which was destroyed by the sea at the end of the fourteenth or beginning of the fifteenth century. The name is one of a number of ON names on the coast (see introduction) – compare *AINSDALE*. Forms such as Bertel, Birthile in records of the seventeenth and eighteenth centuries suggest that the name was still undergoing development then, but the influx of new residents following the opening of the Liverpool-Southport railway-line in 1850 seems to have secured the modern spelling-pronunciation.

Birkland Barrow hill with a birch-tree copse (ON birki + lundr + berg → Birkelundeberh c.1225 → Byrklande Bergh 1451 → Byrklandbargh 16th. c.). The reference is to the hill on which the hamlet stands. ON lundr has become confused with ON and OE land, 'land', in the development of the name.

Birkrig birch-tree ridge (ON birki + hryggr → Byrkeryg 1282), the name of a 400-foot ridge.

Birkwray birch-tree nook (ON birki + vrá → Byrkwray 1600).

Birtle birch-tree hill (OE birce/ON birki + OE hyll → Birkel 1246 → Birkehill 1347 → Birtle 1609).

Bispham the bishop's *hām*, i.e. manor owned by the bishopric (OE biscop + hām), the name of two places:
(1) near Blackpool (Biscopham DB → Bisbhaym c.1270);
(2) parish near Rufford, with no village (Bispam 1219).

Blackburn the black stream (OE blæc + burna → Blachebvrne DB → Blakeburn 1187). The town takes its name from the river on which it stands, now called the *BLACK-WATER*. It also gives its name to one of the county's six hundreds.

Blackley the black *lēah* (OE blæc + lēah → Blakeley 1282 → Blackeley 1577). Examples are for the major name, near Manchester.

Black Moor the black moor (OE blæc + mōr → Blakemor c.1210).

Blacko the black hill (OE blæc + OE hōh/ON haugr → Blacho 12th.c. → Blakhow 1329). The reference is to a 1,018 foot hill to the east of the present village.

Blackpool the black pool (OE blæc + pol → Pul c.1260 → Le Pull 1416 → Blackpoole 1602 → Le poole commonly called Black poole 1637). The name refers to the pool or stream, coloured by the peat, which drained Marton Mere into Spen Dyke and so into the sea, though it is possible that early forms refer rather to the Warton Pool. On Yates' map of 1786 the place is also described as 'Mr Forshaw's Bathing Place'. Modern BLACKPOOL includes South Shore, once an independent village. See also *GYNN, LAYTON*.

Blackrod black clearing (OE blæc + *rod – Blakerode 1201).

Blacksnape ? bleak pasture (OE blāc/ME black + ME snape → Blakesnape 1614). The name is recorded late and etymology is necessarily speculative, but the name refers to a fell-district, making the NCy snape, 'poor pasture', more probable than OE *snæp, 'boggy land', and OE blāc, 'bleak', perhaps more probable than OE blæc, 'black'.

Blackstone Edge the edge with the black stone (OE blæc + stān + ecg → Blakeston Edge Hill 1577). At this 1,269 foot hill the old moor road crosses the county boundary; the name may refer to a black stone used as a boundary-marker.

Blackwater (R) the black river (OE blæc + water → Blak 12th.c.). The stream was apparently known earlier, or alternatively, as the *BLACKBURN*, from which the town takes its name. It sometimes also appears as BLAKEWATER.

Blatchingworth Blæcca's enclosure (OE Blæcca + -n (possessive) + worð → Blackenworthe 1276).

Blawith dark wood (ON blá + viðr → Blawit 1276 → Blawith 1341). This was formerly a forest district.

Bleasdale ? bright valley (ON blesi + dalr → Blesedale 1228). ON blesi means 'white spot on a horse's forehead', but Norw. blesa means 'bare spot on a hillside' and in Swed. dial., the word also has the sense of 'opening between hills'. It is indistinguishable from the ON personal name Blesi, which is also possible here.

Blelham Tarn ? dark pool (ON blá + OE *lumm → Blalam Terne 1537); ON tjǫrn, 'tarn, small lake', has been added. The recorded form is, however, too late for definite etymology.

Blowick dark bay (ON blá + vík → ? le Wyke 1354 → Blowyke 1550 → Blowicke 1602). The earliest form may be Wyke, a minor name in North Meols; Wyke may have been so named because it stood beside Martin Mere, since NCy wyke has the sense of 'small bay in an inland lake'. BLOWICK, to the west, might well require some defining element to distinguish it from Wyke.

Blundellsands The residential district takes its name from the Blundell family of nearby Crosby Hall. See also *INCE BLUNDELL*.

Bold dwelling (OE bold → Bolde 1204). The name is a variant-form of OE bōðl, seen in *BOLTON*; another variant is seen in *BOOTLE*.

Bolton collection of buildings (OE *bōðl-tūn), the name of three places:
(1) BOLTON-LE-MOORS (Boelton 1185 → Bothelton 1212 → Bolton on the Mores 1331), referring to the situation on the moors of south-east Lancashire;
(2) BOLTON-LE-SANDS (Bodeltune DB → Boulton 1206), referring to the situation near the shore of Morecambe Bay. The village gives its name to the self-explanatory BOLTON TOWN END and to BOLTON HOLMES (ON *holmr*, 'higher dry ground among marshes').
(3) LITTLE BOLTON (Bothelton 1212), so called in distinction to BOLTON-LE-MOORS.
The word is confined almost exclusively to the northern counties and has been held to be Northumbrian. It has been suggested that it means 'village proper' as opposed to its outlying land.

Bonds etymology doubtful (Bonds 1667).

Bootle dwelling (OE bōtl → Boltelai DB → Botle 1212). The word is a variation of OE bōðl, seen in *BOLTON*. Another variation is seen in *BOLD* and the earliest form perhaps shows this variation rather than bōtl.

Bordriggs etymology doubtful (Bor-derigges 1330). The second element is ON hryggr, 'ridge', referring to the higher land west of the Kirkby Pool. The first element may be the OE personal name Brorda. OE bord, 'board, plank', seems less probable since it is found usually with terms for woods, but Yates' 1786 map shows the place as Boardridge.

Borwick outlying part of a lord's estate (OE berewīc → Bereuuic DB → Berwik 1228 → Barwyc Hall 1577).

Botton innermost part of the valley (ON botn → Bottun c.1230). The name refers to the area of the upper valley of the R. Hindburn.

Boulsworth Hill the bull's 'neck' (OE *bula/ON boli + OE swēora/ON sviri → Bulswyre pre-14th.c.). Dial. swire has among its meanings 'neck of land, hollow on top of a hill', which would describe the undulations at the top of this 1,700 foot hill. The name has later been re-formed, with the substitution of OE worð, 'enclosure', for swēora.

Bouth herdsman's hut (ONorw buð → Bouthe 1336). The place was originally a dairy-farm belonging to Colton. The form of the name is Norwegian rather than Danish.

Bowland land in a bow (OE boga/ON bogi + OE land/ON land → Boelanda 1102 (Latin) → Bouland c.1140 → Bochlande 1194). The name refers both to a small township in Whalley parish and to a forest area, much of which is in Yorkshire (see introduction p. 30). The exact reference of the name is somewhat obscure, but it has been suggested that 'bow' refers to the bend in the R. Ribble which begins at Bolton-By-Bowland, Yks, and changes the river's course from south to west. Land has the sense of 'tract of land', perhaps indicating the area under forest law.

Boysnope poor pasture grazed by bulls (ON boli + ME snape → Boylsnape 1277).

Bracelet ? broad meadow (ON breiðr + slétta → Bracelet 1614). The earliest recorded form is late and the name may well have been modified through association with the ME loan-word from OF, bracelet, which has no relevance to the meaning of the name.

Bradford wide ford (OE brād + ford → Bradeford 1196).

Bradshaw wide wood (OE brād + sceaga → Bradeshawe 1246).

Brandwood the wood cleared or destroyed by burning (ME brende + OE wudu → Brendewod c.1200).

Brathay (R) the broad river (ON breiðr + á → Braiza, Braitha c.1160 → Brathey 1671). The river forms the county boundary with Westmoreland and is wide in its lower reaches.

Breck slope (ON brekka → Brek 1323).

Breightmet bright meadow (OE beorht + mæd → Brihtsmete 1246 → Brihtmede 1257 → Breghtmete 1323).

Bretherton the brother's *tūn* (ON bróðir, in the form brœðr (possessive sg.) + OE tūn → Bretherton 1190). The form of the first element suggests ON rather than the OE cognate bróðor. Although the precise significance of the reference is uncertain, it is possible that here, as in areas of the Danelaw, the estate was handed over to a younger brother.

Bridgewater Canal The canal takes the name of the Dukes of Bridgewater. It was projected by the first Duke and built by the third Duke in 1759-61.

Briercliffe hill where briers grow (OE brēr + clif → Brerecleve 1193 → Brerclif 1332). The name survives in the parish name, BRIERCLIFFE-WITH-*EXTWISTLE*. Extwistle Hall is on the south bank of the Thursden Brook and clif here probably refers to the steep northern bank. Compare *BRIERFIELD*.

Brierfield There are no early forms available for this cotton-town of the Industrial Revolution – it is not even on Yates' 1786 map – but the name is apparently self-explanatory. Standing on the Leeds-Liverpool Canal, in the valley of the Pendle Water, its location and name contrast with nearby *BRIERCLIFFE*, perhaps with conscious comparison.

Brimmicroft field where broom grows (OE brōmig + croft → Bromicroft 1246 → Bromicroft in Wythenul post-1282).

Brindle hill where there is a stream (OE burna + hyll → Brumhull 1203 → Burnhull 1206 → Brynhill 1480 →

Bryndall 1509). The reference is to The Lostock Brook, which rises here.

Brinscall hut destroyed by fire (ME brende + ON skáli → Brendescoles c.1200 → Brendeschales 1246 → Brinscolls 1670).

Britannia A modern name, which was presumably taken from a local inn. The name presumably dates from the late nineteenth century since, at 967 feet, this is the highest point of the railway line from Rochdale which opened in 1881 and encouraged development at this spot.

Broad Green self-explanatory (Broadgreen 1730).

Broad Oak the large oak-tree (OE brād + āc → Brode Oke 1589). The reference may be to an oak-tree used as a boundary marker or meeting place.

Brock (R) stream (OE brōc → Brock c.1200).

Brooksbottom valley of the stream (OE brōc + -es (possessive) + botm). The name refers to the wooded gorge of the R. Irwell. There are no early forms – the name was clearly a minor name until the hamlet grew up around the cotton mill built here by John Robinson Kay in 1829.

Broughton tūn by a stream (OE brōc + tūn), the name of five places:
(1) near Preston, by the Blundel Brook (Broctun DB → Broghton 1303);
(2) BROUGHTON-IN-*CARTMEL*, on the R. Eea (Brocton 1276).

The name is preserved in the hamlets of FIELD BROUGHTON and WOOD BROUGHTON, and in the parish-name of BROUGHTON EAST, so-called in distinction to (3) below;
(3) BROUGHTON-IN-*FURNESS*, near the estuary of the R. Duddon, south of the ridge between the Kirkby Pool and the R. Lickle (Brocton 1196). The parish is BROUGHTON WEST;
(4) BROUGHTON BECK (Broctunebec c.1246), also called BROUGHTON in early records (Broghton 1332), took its name from the stream on which it stands. The stream was then called by the name of the hamlet, and ON bekkr, 'stream', was added. The word beck was then added also to the hamlet-name to distinguish it from (3) above:
(5) BROUGHTON -ON - *IRWELL* must be distinguished from the other four in having a different etymology, '*burh* with *tūn*' (OE burh + tūn → Burton 1177). The change in the position of the -r- is more likely to be the result of normal linguistic tendencies than to be the result of mistaken etymology caused by the proximity of the site to the R. Irwell.

Brownside land by the R. *BRUN* (*BRUN* + OE sīde). Compare the 1469 form under *BRUN* below.

Brun (R) the brown river (OE brūn → Brun c.1200 → Browne 1469). This is presumably the same element as the first element in *BROWNSIDE, BRUNSHAW* and *BURNLEY*. Another possibility is that it is a variant form of OE burna, 'stream'.

Brunshaw copse by the R. *BRUN* (BRUN + OE sceaga → Brunschaghe 1296). It is, however, possible that brūn here could be used adjectively, meaning 'brown'.

Bryn hill (Welsh bryn → Brunne 1276 → Bryn 1430), a name indicative of Celtic influence (see introduction p. 36).

Bryning etymology doubtful (Bir staf Brinn(ing) 1201 → Birstatbrunning 1236 → Brining 1243). The early forms have ON bjarstaðr, 'farmstead', as the first element. The place is on the flat northern bank of the estuary of the R. Ribble. Two possibilities have been suggested — that the name derives from OE burna, 'stream', with the formative place-name suffix -ing, meaning 'place associated with a stream' and thus referring to the R. Ribble; and that the name consists of the OE personal name Brȳni with the suffix -ingas and means 'the people associated with Brȳni'. By the latter etymology, the name would be a folk-name, indicative of early Anglo-Saxon settlement (see introduction p. 37).

Buckley bucks' *lēah* (OE bucc + lēah → Bukele 1246). Lēah clearly has the sense of 'clearing' here.

Buersil etymology doubtful (?Brideshull 1228 → Berdeshull 1292 → Burdssell More 1543). The second element is clearly OE hyll, 'hill'. On the basis of the earliest form, the meaning 'Bridd's hill', from the OE personal name Bridd + -es (possessive) has been proposed, but it is not certain that the form refers to this place. Another possible first element

suggested is OE *byrđe, 'border, edge, bank'.

Bulk hill (ON bulki → Bulk 1313).

Burnage ? brown hedge (OE brūn + hegge → Bronadge 1322 → Bronnegge 1322).

Burnden valley where the stream flows (OE burna + denu → Bornden 1285 → Brunden 1332). The site is on the R. Croal and is probably best known as the name of the ground of Bolton Wanderers Association Football Club (1894).

Burnley *lēah* on the R. *BRUN* (BRUN + OE lēah → Brunlaia 1124 (Latin) → Bronley 1258 → Burneley 1433 → Burneley al. Brunley 1533).

Burrow *burh* (OE burh → Borch DB → Burg 1212 → Burgo c.1240). The name appears in OVER BURROW and NETHER BURROW (Overburgh, Nethirburgh 1370), the survivors of two manors. The name may refer to a Roman encampment near OVER BURROW; a Roman road runs along the eastern boundary of the township.

Burscough wood by a *burh* (OE burh + ON skógr → Burgechou c.1190 → Burscogh c.1190). The name appears also in BURSCOUGH BRIDGE, a bridge over the Mill Goit.

Burtonwood wood belonging to BURTON (BURTON + OE wudu → Burtoneswod 1228 → Bourtonewood 1251). The name BURTON (OE burh-tūn → Burton 1200), 'enclosure round a *burh*', has been lost. This dependent manor of Warrington was taken into the royal forest by Henry I.

Bury (at) the *burh* (OE burh, in the form byrig (dative) → Biri 1194 → Bury c.1190).

Butterworth the 'butter-worð', i.e. the enclosed pasture-land that produces good butter (OE butere + worð → Buterwrth ·1235 → Butterwurth 1246).

C

Cabus etymology doubtful (Kaibal c.1205 → Caybel 1246 → Caboos c.1550). The earliest forms suggest that the second element is OE *ball, 'rounded hill, hillock', also used in the sense 'mound of earth set up as a boundary mark'. The first element is less certain; an OE personal name *Cæg/*Cæga, and OE cæg, 'key', in an earlier sense of 'peg', have been proposed. The name is that of a villageless parish in the Fylde, and recurs in the later hamlet-name, CABUS NOOK, on the Lancaster Canal within the parish. There is thus little precise topographical indication of the name's reference, although perhaps the sense of 'boundary-marker' may be preferred. The later development of the name perhaps shows substitution of OE *bōs, 'cowstall', as second element.

Cadishead animal-fold by the stream called CADWALE (CADWALE + OE (ge) set → Cadwalesate 1212 → Cadewalleheved 1322 → Cadyswalhede 1538). The first part of the name is a lost stream-name, ending in OE wella', 'stream', whose first element is no longer traceable, although it may be a personal name or hill-name. The final element has been confused with and replaced by 'head', from OE hēafod.

Cadley etymology doubtful, although the second element is clearly OE *lēah* (Cadileisale 1228 → Cadilegh 1314).

Cadshaw Cada's spur (OE Cada + hōh → Kaddehou c.1200/Cadeshoubroc c.1200). The ending has been confused with OE sceaga, 'wood, copse'.

Calder, (R) the rocky stream (Welsh caled + Celt *dubro-). Caled means 'hard', and 'violent, rapid' has also been suggested as its reference here. Two rivers bear this name:
(1) the 'two-forked CALDER', with two head-streams which meet at Burnley (Caldre 1193);
(2) tributary of the R. Wyre (Keldir

c.1200 → Caldre c.1220).

Cant Beck (R) etymology doubtful (Kant 1202). It may be a back formation from *CANTSFIELD* or be Celt. *canto-; the meaning of the latter is, however, obscure, although a sense 'brilliant' has been proposed for this name, as has 'loud'.

Cantsfield ?open country by the R. *CANT* (CANT + -es (possessive) + OE feld → Cantesfelt DB → Canceveld 1202). Much depends upon the etymology of the river-name, but it has been argued that since the village is south of the CANT BECK, on a tributary, the first element could be an OE personal name, *Cant, from Canta, a shortened form of some compound name such as Cantwine, + -es (possessive), and the river-name back-formed from this. Possibly, however, the R. CANT gave its name to the tongue of land formed by the junction of the rivers Lune and Greeta as the most distinctive form of reference.

Capernwray chapman's valley (ON kaup-maðr, in the form kaup-manna (possessive) + vrá → Coupmanwra c.1200 → Koupemoneswra 1212 → Copynwra c.1350 → Capanwray 1509 → Capernwray 1767). The village is in the valley of the R. Keer at a point where the land on either side of the river rises. There is a river crossing here.

Cark rock (OWelsh carrec → Karke 1491). This is the only Celtic major name in Cartmel (see introduction p.26).

Carleton *tūn* owned by a freeman of the rank of 'ceorl' (ON karl + OE tūn → Carlentun DB → Carlton 1190). The name may well have had as first element OE ceorl, 'peasant', originally; it has been suggested as likely that "a *ceorla-tūn* was land on the outskirts of an estate taken for cultivation, fenced and allocated to peasants" (EPNE).

Carnforth heron ford (OE cran + ford → Chreneforde DB → Carneford 1212 → Carnforth 1577). The village is near the R. Keer at the point at which the river-valley opens into Morecambe Bay. The development of unstressed '-rd' to '-rth' is frequent in NCy '-ford' names.

Cartmel sandbank by rocky ground (ON *kartr + melr → Ceartmel, Cartmel 12th. c.). The village is on the R. Eea with a ridge of high land to the east reaching 616 feet at Fell End. Some influence from OE cert, 'rough ground', may be seen in the Ceartmel form. The place may be Cherchebi in DB (OE cirice + ON bȳ), and it appears also as Churchtowne in 1585, although Saxton shows it as Cartmell in 1577. The village contains the priory founded in 1188 by William Marshall, Earl of Pembroke, whose large church would reinforce the 'Churchtown' name. CARTMEL is the name of the district of the Cartmel Peninsula and as far north as the east shore of Windermere where it gives its name to CARTMEL FELL (CARTMEL + ON fjall → Cartmelfell 1537), the fell-land on the eastern shore of Windermere and also a hamlet-name.

Castleton *tūn* by a castle (ONFr castel + OE tūn → Castelton 1246). The place is said to be named from a castle on the R. Roch near the church, recorded as 'Villa Castelli de Racheham'. The name would then be post-Conquest.

Caton Catta's *tūn* (OE Catta + tūn → Catun DB).

Catshaw copse where the wildcat lives (OE cat(t) + sceaga → Cattesagh 1323 → Catteshawe 1324).

Catterall etymology doubtful (Catrehala DB → Caterhale 1212 → Cateral c.1220). Within the parish the rivers Calder and Brock flow into the R. Wyre and the village is near the junction of the former. OE *halh*, 'water-meadow', has at least influenced the second element and would be appropriate; the first element would then be an OE personal name, Cater. But ON kattarhali, 'cat's tail', has been strongly suggested by scholars.

Caw Hill calf (OE calf → Calfheud c.1177), in the sense of 'small hill' in comparison to the other hills of the northern group. The height is 1,735 feet. In the c.1177 form, OE hēafod, 'hill', has been added.

Cawood jackdaw wood (OE *cā + wudu → Kawode c.1205). CAWOOD was the forest of the lords of Melling and survives in the parish-name of *ARKHOLME*-WITH-CAWOOD.

Chadderton ?*tūn* on or by a hill (OWelsh *cadeir + OE tūn → Chaderton c.1200). *Cadeir, normally 'chair', is sometimes used to refer to a hill or eminence but this cannot be said to be its sense in all place-names.

Chadwick Ceadda's *wīc* (OE Ceadda + wīc → Chaddewyk c.1180). The parish church of Rochdale, to the east, is dedicated to St. Chad, which may explain the first element; if so, wīc probably means 'hamlet, village'.

Chaigley Ceadda's *lēah* (OE Ceadda + lēah → Chadelegh 1246 → Chaidesley 1336 → Chadgeley 1391 → Chawgeley 1437 → Chageley 1514). The name's development may have been influenced by OE *ceacga, 'broom, gorse, brushwood', which would give good sense in context.

Chapel Island This island in mid-channel of the Leven estuary takes its name from a chapel used by travellers across the Leven Sands with their guides, the monks of Cartmel or Conishead.

Charnock Richard ? stone (Brit. *carn + -āco → Chernoch 1194 → Chernok Ricard 1288). If the above etymology is accepted, the Celt. root may describe either the district or a river (e.g. the Yarrow) – 'stony ground' or 'river with stony bed'. To this name has been added that of the local family, Richard de Charnock, to distinguish it from *HEATH CHARNOCK*.

Chatburn Ceatta's stream (OE Ceatta + burna → Chatteburn 1242). The village is on a small brook near the Ribble. An OE ceat, 'piece of wet ground', proposed for *CHAT MOSS*, would give sense here also.

Chat Moss Ceatta's swamp (OE Ceatta + mos → Catemosse 1277 → Chatmos 1322). It has been suggested that the first element may be an OE ceat, 'piece of wet ground'.

71

Chatterton ? *tūn* on a hill (Pr Welsh *cadeir + OE tūn → Chatterton 1523). Compare *CHADDERTON*, which presents the same problems with the first element.

Cheesden gravel-valley (OE *cis + denu → Chesden Water 1543).

Cheetham *hām* in a wood (Brit. *cēto + OE hām → Chetam 1212). It is probable that the first element was regarded as a name before the second was added. Compare *CHEETWOOD*.

Cheetwood wood called CHEET (Brit. *cēto- + OE wudu → Chetewode 1489). Here Brit. *cēto-, 'wood', was clearly regarded as a name without lexical meaning when OE wudu was added. Since CHEETWOOD is about a mile south of *CHEETHAM*, the reference of both names is probably the same.

Cherry Tree The name is self-explanatory, but may have become the name of a settlement through extension from an inn-name. 'The Cherry Tree at Livesey' is recorded in c.1850.

Chesham at the gravelly places (OE *cis + -um (dative pl) → Chesum 1429).

Childwall child's stream (OE cild + wella → Cildeuuelle DB → Childewell 1094 → Childewalle 1212). The form of the second element varies between Merc. wælla, source of the modern form, and Nhb. wella – the name appears as Childwell as late as 1732. The first element has been much debated, and the OE personal name Cilda and the OE celde,

'spring', specifically in the sense here of 'sudden burst of water from a hill', have been proposed; the latter may derive some support from the high ridge on which CHILDWALL stands. Cild, proposed here, would perhaps indicate a stream that a child could cross.

Chipping market-place (OE cēping → Chippin 1203 → Chypping 1241).

Chippingdale market-place valley (OE cēping + ON dalr → Chipinden DB → Cepndela 1102 (Latin) → Chepyndale 1316).

Chor (R) a brook in *CHORLEY* from which the name is back-formed; it is first recorded in 1673 but was known as the Main Brook, the brook which marked the edge of the demesne land (ME main).

Chorley *lēah* belonging to those freeman with the rank of 'ceorl' (OE ceorl + lēah → Cherleg 1246 → Cherlegh 1251 → Chorleye 1304). *Lēah* probably here has the sense of 'meadow-land' rather than 'forest clearing' in view of the location between two rivers.

Chorlton *tūn* belonging to those freemen with the rank of 'ceorl' (OE ceorl + tūn). Two Manchester suburbs bear this name:
(1) CHORLTON-UPON-*MEDLOCK* (Cherleton 1177);
(2) CHORLTON - CUM - HARDY (Cholreton 1243 → Chorleton 1551) – the earliest forms have led to the suggestion that this may be OE Ceol, an abbreviation of some OE compound-name such as Ceolferþ.

Chowbent gorge where bent-grass grows (OE ceole + beonet → Cholale 1323 → Chollebynt c.1350→Chowebent c.1550). The earliest form suggests a possible compound with *lēah*. The OE personal name Ceola has also been suggested as a possible first element.

Church church (OE cirice → Chirche 1202 → Chuchkyrk 1536). The name probably refers to a church on or near the site of the present St. James' Church which is still called locally 'Church Kirk', as it often has been since the sixteenth century.

Churchtown *tūn*, or part of the town, by the church. Two places bear this name:
(1) in *KIRKLAND* parish, containing the church of St. Helen, the old church of Garstang (Church Town 1786);
(2) in Southport, the modern name for *NORTH MEOLS*, referring to the part of the settlement around the church of St. Cuthbert, on the site of an earlier church (Church Town c.1725).
Churchtown was another name for *CARTMEL*.

Claife steep hill-side (ON kleif → Clayf c.1275), describing the steep westbank of Lake Windermere.

Claughton *tūn* on or by a hill (OE *clacc + tūn). The name of two places:
(1) in Amounderness, near Garstang (Clactune DB → Clatton 1246 → Clahton 1252 → Claghton 1285). The reference may be to the 250-foot spur of land above the R. Brock, although the land in

the parish rises overall from under 50 feet in the south-west to over 700 feet in the north-east;
(2) in Lonsdale (Clactun DB → Clahton 1208 → Claghton 1297), in the valley of the Lune at the foot of CLAUGHTON MOOR which rises to 1185 feet.
ON klakkr, 'lump, hill', has also been suggested for the first element; the meaning would be unchanged.

Clayton *tūn* on clay soil (OE clæg + tūn). The name of three places:
(1) CLAYTON-LE-DALE (Clayton 1246 → Claiton in the Dale 1327), with the addition of ON dalr, 'valley' — the name of a parish on the south of the R. Ribble (cf. *WALTON-LE-DALE*);
(2) CLAYTON-LE-MOORS (Cleyton 1243 → Clayton super Moras 1284), with the addition of OE mōr + -as (pl), 'high tract of barren land' — the high land between Accrington and Great Harwood;
(3) CLAYTON-LE-WOODS(Claiton c.1200), with OE wudu, 'wood' (cf. *WHITTLE-LE-WOODS* to the south-east) — name of a parish on the valley of the R. Lostock and of CLAYTON GREEN, a hamlet within the parish.
The three places are quite close to each other and the suffixes are particularly necessary to identify the places clearly. On LE, see introduction p.43.

Clegg hill(ON kleggi→Clegg c.1200). The name may refer to Owl Hill, at the foot of which CLEGG stands.

Clerk Hill (Clerkhill 1517), the southern spur of Pendle Hill, formerly Snelleshowe 1296, 'Sniall's hill' (ON Sniallr + haugr).

Cleveley Bank *lēah* by a cliff (OE clif + lēah → Cliueleie c.1180 → Cliueley c.1270). The reference is to rising ground to the west of the R. Wyre near Forton. On the other side of the same rise is the hamlet of Clifton Hill, with comparable first element. See *CLIFTON*.

Clifton *tūn* on or by a slope (OE clif + tūn → Clistun DB → Clifton 1226). The forms quoted are for the CLIFTON, parish and hamlet-name, of Amounderness. The reference is to the northern bank of the R. Ribble which formerly flowed much closer to the village than today, covering the present CLIFTON MARSH. The name is, however, frequent as a minor name.

Clitheroe hill of loose stones (OE *clȳder + ON haugr → Cliderhou 1102 → Clitherow 1124). The town, one of the new towns of the Middle Ages, was planted beside the castle (held in 1100 by Robert de Lacy). It takes its name from the hill on which the castle stands which, being of limestone, is loose and crumbling. OE hōh, 'spur', has been proposed as second element.

Cliviger cultivated land by a slope (OE clif + æcer → Cliuercher 1196 → Clyuacher 1246 → Clyfacre 1311 → Clyuycher 1558). The township includes the steep banks of the R. Calder. The '-g-' is pronounced as '-j-', a development often held to be a Mercian form (see introduction p. 39).

Cocker (R) the crooked river (Celt.

*kukrā → Cocur ?930 → Cokir c.1155), referring to the winding course of the stream across the flat mossland from Winmarleigh to the R. Lune.

Cockerham *hām* on the R. *COCKER* (COCKER + OE hām → Cocreham DB → Kokerham 1190).

Cockersand the sands at the mouth of the R. *COCKER* (COCKER + OE sand → Cocresha 1207 → Kokersand 1212), the site of COCKERSAND Abbey.

Cockshotts Wood cock-shoot wood – i.e. woodland area where nets were spread to catch woodcock (OE *cocc-scīete → Cokeshoteslace 1380 → Cockshot Wood 1539), name of a wood south of Melling, Lonsdale.

Coldcoats cheerless huts (OE cald + cot + -as (pl.)→ Kaldecotes 1243 → Coldecotes 1279). At a height of 481 feet on the Whalley-Pendleton road, at the foot of a steep moorside, the location suggests that the huts were 'shelters for travellers' and cald perhaps suggests their exposed position.

Colloway etymology doubtful. If the form Collingeswelle c.1200 represents the ancestor of the modern name, 'Colling's stream' (OE Colling + -es (possessive) + wella) would be the meaning, but the development would be difficult to establish.

Collyhurst charcoal copse (OE *colig + hyrst → Colyhurst 1322).

Colne ? roaring river (Celt. *colauno- → Coune 1292). The sense of the Celt. term, found in a number of river-names, is doubtful. The COLNE WATER gave its name to the town of COLNE (Calna 1124 → Kaun 1242 → Colne 1296), 'place on the R. COLNE'.

Colton tūn on the R. Cole (COLE + OE tūn → Coleton 1202 → Colton 1332). The reference is to the COLTON BECK, now 'stream on which COLTON stands' (COLTON + ON bekkr), but originally called the R. Cole 'the hazel stream' (Welsh coll → Cole 1247).

Conder (R) the crooked stream (Celt. *cambo- + *dubro- → Kondover c.1200 → Kondoure c.1240 → Condofre 1292 → Condar c.1540), descriptive of the river's course in the flat land between Quernmore and Glasson (cf. R. *COCKER*). CONDER GREEN takes its name from the river.

Conishead the king's headland (ON konungr + OE hēafod → Cuningesheued c.1182 → Conigeshevede c.1182 → Kunisheved 1245). The name is probably entirely OE in origin, the first element being OE cyning + -es (possessive) which has later been replaced by the ON form. The reference is to a headland overlooking the Ulverston Sands, site of a priory of Augustinian canons and terminus of a sands-crossing (cf. Saxton's 'Conyside passage' 1577). Names in cyning often refer to royal manors or estates.

Coniston the king's tūn (ON konungr + OE tūn → Coningeston c.1160). The ON element may have replaced OE cyning + -es (possessive) (cf. *CONISHEAD*). Names in cyning often refer to royal manors or estates. The lake, CONISTON WATER, takes its name from the town; it was formerly Thurston Water (Turstiniwatra c.1160 → Thurstainewater 1196), 'Thorsteinn's lake'.

Coppull peaked hill (OE copp + hyll → Cophill 1218 → Cophul c.1234 → Coppull c.1429). The village is on a slight plateau.

Corner Row crane island (OE corn + ēg → Cornege 1189 → Cornoe 13th.c. → Cornoe Row 13th.c. → Corneraw 1501). The hamlet is to the west of an arm of the Thistleton Brook and the name may refer to the slightly higher land between the two arms of the Brook. Although the first element could be OE corn, 'corn', the topography makes 'crane' more probable.

Cottam (at) the cottages (OE cot + -um (dative pl.) → Cotun 1230 → Cotum c.1235).

Cowan Bridge Colling's bridge (OE Colling + brycg → Collingbrigke c.1200), a hamlet at a bridging-point of the R. Lune.

Cowpe cow valley (OE cū + hop → Cuhope c.1200). The hamlet stands on a brook, in a valley to the south of the main valley of the R. Irwell. On COWPE SCAR, see *COWPREN POINT*.

Cowpren Point etymology doubtful (Gowborn head 1577). The name of this coastal promontory in south-west Cartmel may have influenced, or been influenced by, that of another headland, COWPE SCAR, to the south-east. The etymology of the latter cannot be the same as *COWPE* above.

Crake (R) the rocky stream (OWelsh *creic → Crayke c.1160).

Crawshaw Booth wood where crows are found (OE crāwe + sceaga → Croweshagh 1324 → Crawshaboth 1507). ODan. bōth, with the sense of 'dairy farm', has been added to the existing place-nàme.

Crimbles small piece(s) of land (OE *crymel → Crimeles DB → Crimblis c.1155 → Crimbles 1207), name of two hamlets, GREAT and LITTLE CRIMBLES.

Cringlebarrow Wood wood on a circular hill (ON kringla + OE beorg → Cringelborhanes c.1250). The earliest form shows the addition of OE nes, 'headland'.

Cringle Brook (R) the twisting stream (OE *cringol/ ON kringla + brōc → Kryngelbroke 1322).

Croal (R) the winding stream (OE crōh + wella). The river is the Middlebrook (OE mycel + brōc → Mikelbrok 1292), 'the great stream', above Bolton, and it has been suggested that this was formerly the name of the whole length of river, hence the absence of early forms of CROAL.

Croft small field (OE croft → Croft 1212).

Crompton *tūn* in a bend (OE crumb + tūn → Crumpton 1246 → Crompton 1246).

Cronton crows' *tūn* (OE crāwe + -na (possessive pl.) + tūn → Crohinton 1242 → Crouington 1246 → Crounton c.1250 → Crointon 1332).

Crook land in the bend of a river (ON krókr → Crokispul c.1160 → Croc 1190). The forms given are for the hamlet on the coast, in a bend of the Lune estuary, but the element recurs in minor names – e.g. CROOK, near Shevington (Crok 1324).

Crosby *býr* with crosses (ON krossbýr/krossa-býr → Crosebi DB). The name of two neighbouring villages, GREAT CROSBY (Magnum Crossby c.1190 → Great Crosseby 1246) and LITTLE CROSBY (Parua Crosseby c.1260 → Little Crosseby 1243). Six stone crosses still remain at LITTLE CROSBY.

Crossens headland on which a cross or crosses stand(s) (OIr cros/ON kross/lOE cros + ON nes → Crosseness 1240 → Crossons 1550). The hamlet is on a promontory at the mouth of the Ribble.

Croston *tūn* with a cross (OIr cros/ON kross/lOE cros + OE tūn → Croston 1094). Part of the market cross still remains.

Croxteth Krókr's landing-place (ON Krókr + stọð → Crocstad 1257 → Croxstath 1297).

Crumpsall water-meadow belonging to Crum (OE Crum + -es (possessive) + halh → Cormeshal 1235 → Cromshall 1548). The site lies in a large bend of the R. Irk. OE crumb, 'bend', is a tempting derivation for the first element, but would leave the '-s-' unexplained.

Cuerdale etymology doubtful (Kiuerdale c.1190→Keuerdale 1282 → Curedale 1374). The second element is clearly ON dalr, 'valley', referring to the valley of the R. Ribble. Various suggestions have been made to explain the first element — the OE personal name Cynferþ and an OE *cyfrede + halh, 'rounded valley' — but none is convincing.

Cuerden ? ash-tree (Welsh cerddin → Kerden c.1200), presumably retained because of the similarity of the ending to OE denu, 'valley'; the site is in a bend of the R. Lostock. But 'Cær's valley' (OE Cær + denu) has also been suggested.

Cuerdley etymology doubtful (Kyuerlay 1246 → Keuerdeley 1282 → Keerdelegh 1344). The second element is clearly OE lēah, but a postulated OE *cyfrede, 'rounded', and the OE personal name Cynferþ, which have been tentatively proposed as first elements, do not seem convincing.

Culcheth narrow wood (Welsh cul + coed → Culchet 1201 → Culchith 1284).

Cunscough the king's wood (ODan kunung + ON skógr → Cunigescofh 1190 → Cunsco 1300).

Cunsey ? king's river/'island' (ODan. kunung + -s (possessive) + á/ey → Concey Myll 1537). Lack of early forms makes derivation tentative.

D

Daisy Nook See *WATERHOUSES*.

Dalton tūn in a valley (ON dalr + OE tūn). Name of four places in Lancashire:
(1) nr. Wigan, at the foot of Ashhurst Beacon (Daltone DB → Dalton 1212);
(2) DALTON LEES, 'the meadows belonging to DALTON' (DALTON + OE lēah, in the form lēas (pl.)), taking its name from nearby DALTON (1);

(3) near Burton in Kendal, referring to the valley north of Dalton Hall (Dalton 1225);
(4) DALTON-IN-*FURNESS* (Daltune DB → Dalton in Fournais 1332), referring to the valley, enclosed by hills, in which the town stands.

Damas Gill (R) lake of the doe by the ravine (OE dā + mere + ON gil → Dameresgile/Damesgile 1228). There is a tarn, now a ·reservoir,

77

near the stream.

Darcy Lever See *LEVER*.

Darwen river where oak-trees grow (Brit. *derventjū). The name first applied to the river (Derewente 1227 → Derwyn 1560) and was then applied to the town, which stands in a cleft between the moors through which the river flows. The town comprises the two villages of OVER DARWEN (Overderewęnte 1216) and LOWER DARWEN (Netherderwent 1311), but is recorded as a single community also (Derewent 1208 → Darrun 1868). A record of 1656 indicates that at that time the river had the alternative name of 'Moulding Water'.

Davyhulme the lonely *hulm* (ON daufligr + ODan. hulm → Hulme 1276 → Dewhulm 1313 → Defèhulme 1434 → Devaholme 1577). The first element has been kept in distinction to nearby *HULME, LEVENSHULME, RUSHOLME*, (see introduction, p.45), but has been corrupted by association with the abbreviated personal-name 'Davy'.

Deane valley, esp. deep wooded valley of stream (OE denu → Dene 1292). Although the form given here is of the village south-west of Bolton, the same element occurs in many minor names in the county.

Dearnley hidden *lēah* (OE derne + lēah → Dernylegh 1324 → Derneley 1581). Derne is usually used with words for 'river' or 'ford'.

Deerslack flat ground on which deer are found (ON dýr + slétta → Dures-slet 1324); the second element has later been replaced by OWScand. slakki, 'valley'.

Dendron clearing in a valley (OE denu + ON rúm → Dene DB → Denrum 1269 → Dendron 1584). The village stands in a valley by a small brook. The second element is found mainly in northern placenames.

Denton *tūn* in a valley (OE denu + tūn → Denton 1255). The reference is apparently to the slight valley in which a small brook flows. Similar references to low-lying land can be seen in nearby *GORTON* to the west and *HAUGHTON* to the east. Although OE Dena tūn, 'Danes' *tūn*', can safely be rejected as an etymology, it is possible that the confusion of Dena and denu is reflected in Dane Bank to the south.

Derby, West See *WEST DERBY*.

Dewhurst wood in damp ground (OE dēaw + hyrst → le Deuyhurst 1284 → Deuhurst c.1300).

Didsbury Dyddi's *burh* (OE *Dyddi (deriv. of Dudd/Dudda) + burh, in the form byrig (dative) → Dedesbiry 1246 → Diddesbiri 1260).

Dilworth dill/vetch enclosure (OE dile + worð → Bileuurde DB → Dilworth 1227).

Dimple pit (OE *dumpel/*dympel – no early examples).

Dinckley *lēah* by the 'fort in the wood' (Celt. *dūno-/OWelsh din + *cēto- + OE lēah), a Celtic placename to which an OE explanatory suffix was later added (Dunky-thele 1246 → Dinkedelay 1246 → Dynkeley 1311). The parish comprises an area of meadows and pasture-land south of the R. Ribble.

Dinckling Green valley (ME dingle + OE grene → Denglegrene 1462). GREEN, 'village green', is a late addition.

Dineley *lēah* on slope (OE dyne + lēah → Dynley 1296).

Dingle deep dell (ME dingle → Dingyll 1246). The village is situated round a former creek.

Ditton *tūn* with ditch (OE dīc + tūn → Ditton 1194). The reference is probably to a drainage ditch in this low-lying land near the R. Mersey. Compare *UPTON*, on higher land to the north.

Docker ? hut in a hollow (ON dǫkk + erg → Dokker 1505). Earlier forms are needed to make etymology certain.

Dolphinholme Dolgfinn's *holmr* (ON Dolgfinnr + holmr → Dolphineholme 1591). The name 'Dolfin' is frequent in the north in the eleventh century. Compare *DOLPHINLEE*.

Dolphinlee Dolgfinn's *lēah* (ON Dolgfinnr + OE lēah → Dolfenlee 1533). On the personal name, see *DOLPHINHOLME*.

Don (R) ? river (Celt. *dānā – no early forms).

Douglas (R) the black stream (Celt. *dubo- + *glassjo- → Duglas 1147). The lower reaches of the river below

Tarleton are also known as R. *ASLAND*.

Dovecot The name is self-explanatory, but was extended to the area from the name of Dovecot House (Dovecoat House 1710) in Pilch Lane which was demolished in the eighteenth century.

Dowbridge valley bridge (OE dæl/ ON dalr + OE brycg → Dalebrige 1268). The stream in the valley is called the DOW – perhaps a back-formation from the place-name.

Downham (at) the hills (OE dūn + -um (dative pl) → Dunum 1188 → Dunham 1246 → Dounham 1294). The village is on a ridge-slope with several hills nearby, of which the most obvious is Pendle.

Downholland the lower 'Holland', as opposed to *UPHOLLAND*; land on a spur (OE dūne + hōh + land → Holand DB → Dounholond 1292). The village is on the slope of a 77-foot ridge in flat country.

Downlitherland See *LITHERLAND*.

Droylesden valley of the dry stream (OE 'drȳge-welle' + -s (possessive) + denu → Drilisden c.1250 → Drils-den c.1290 → Droylsden 1786). 'drȳge-welle' would develop as a name, perhaps referring to a stream which was dry in summer, and the final element would then be added to the stream-name.

Duckworth duck-enclosure (OE dūce + worþ → Ducworth 1241).

Duddel Dudda's hill (OE Dudda + hyll → Dodehill 1324 → Duddill

1590). The first element is the same as that of *DUTTON*. The brook flowing through Dutton is called both the Duddel Brook and the Dutton Brook.

Duddon (R) etymology doubtful (Dudun 1140 → Doden c.1292).

Dumplington *tūn* by a pool (OE *dympel + -ing + tūn → Dumplinton 1229).

Dunnerdale valley of the R. *DUDDON* (DUDDON, in the ON form duðnar (possessive pl.) + dalr → Dunerdal 1293). The reference is to a ten-mile long valley east of the R. DUDDON. The first element is seen also in the minor name, DUNNERHOLME, (duðnar + holmr), 'the land by the R. DUDDON', on the DUDDON estuary. See also *SEATHWAITE*.

Dunnockshaw hedge-sparrow wood (OE dunnoc + sceaga → Dunnockschae 1296), suiting its location in the Forest of Rossendale.

Dunscar dung marsh (OE dynge + ON kjarr → Dungecarre 12th. c. → Dundgecarr 1622).

Dutton Dudda's *tūn* (OE Dudda + tūn → Dotona 1102 (Latin) → Dutton c.1185). See also *DUDDEL*.

Duxbury ? Dēowuc's *byrh* (OE Dēowuc + -es (possessive) + burh, in the form byrig (dative) → Deukesbiri 1202 → Dukesbiri 1227 → Duxbury 1506).

Dwerryhouse dwarf's house (OE dwerg + hūs → Dwery houses clyf mid-13th. c. → Dwerihouse 1332).

E

Earlestown The town developed in 1826-30 around the wagon-works of the railway, and stands on the Liverpool-Manchester line. It was named after Sir Hardman Earle, director of the Liverpool and Manchester Railway Company.

Earnshaw Earn's *halh* (OE Earn + -es (possessive) + halh → Erneshagh 14th.c.). The hamlet is by the River Lostock.

Eastham the east *holmr* (OE ēast + ON holmr → Estholme c.1190). The hamlet is in low-lying ground, and probably stood originally on an area of firm ground in the surrounding moss.

Eaves edge of a wood (OE efes). The word is a common element in major and minor names; cf. (1) nr. Chorley (Euese 1288); (2) nr. St. Michael's-on-Wyre (Eves 1538).

Eccles church (Lat. ecclesia → 1 Brit. *eglēs → Eccles c.1200). The name indicates a Celtic settlement – the town evidently grew up around its church.

Eccleshill ? church hill (Lat. ecclesia → 1 Brit. *eglēs + OE hyll → Eccleshull 1246 → Eccleshill 1322). The hill seems to have been a nearby spur, 860 feet high. There is, however, no trace or record of an early church here.

Eccleston church *tūn* (Lat. ecclesia → 1 Brit. *eglēs + OE tūn). The name of four villages:
(1) nr. Prescot (Ecclistona 1190 (Latin) → Ecclistona in Derbissyre c.1260);
(2) nr. Chorley (Aycleton 1094 → Ecclestun c.1180).
Two other villages are also distinguished as
(3) GREAT ECCLESTON (Egleston DB → Hecliston late 13th.c. → Eclyston Magna 1306); and
(4) LITTLE ECCLESTON (Eglestun DB).
The first element suggests Celtic settlement.

Edenbreck ? slope by river (Brit. *itunā + ON brekka → Etenbreck 1285). The exact meaning of Brit. *itunā is not known; the name refers to a district of Lancaster.

Edenfield field belonging to the island *tūn* (OE ēg + tūn + feld → Aytounfeld 1324 → Etenfelde 1591

→ Edenfeld 1615). The name is probably late, since 'ēgtūn' must have been established as a place-name before 'feld' was added.

Edgworth enclosure on a hillside (OE ecg + worþ → Eggewrthe 1212 → Eggeworth 1276).

Eea (R) river (ON á). There are no early forms. See also *AYSIDE*.

Egerton The town was probably named after the Egerton family who previously owned the land.

Egton *tūn* on an edge (OE ecg + tūn → Egetona 1298 (Latin) → Egetun 1262). The name survives only in the parish-name EGTON-WITH-NEWLAND. It has been suggested that the village may have been near Penny Bridge, where the hills descend to the R. Crake. An alternative etymology, sometimes preferred because '-g-' is here pronounced '-k-', is 'Ecga's tūn' (OE Ecga + tūn).

Ellel Ella's *halh* (OE Ella + halh → Ellhale DB → Ellale 1212 → Ellell 1451). *halh* probably means 'water-meadow', referring to the situation by the R. Conder.

Eller Beck (R) alder-tree beck (ON elri + bekkr → Ellerbek 1246).

Elmers Green The hamlet appears on Yates' 1786 map as Elmhouse Green, which, if reflecting the original form, would suggest a self-explanatory minor name.

Elston Æthel's *tūn* (OE Æþel + -es (possessive) + tūn → Etheliston 1212 → Hetleston pre-1246 → Elston 1423). The first element is a shortened form of some OE personal name such as Æþelsige.

Elswick Æthelsige's *wīc* (OE Æþelsige + -s (possessive) + wīc → Edelesuuic DB → Hedthelsiwic c.1160 → Ethelswic 1202 → Elswike 1567). ELSWICK LEYS, a hamlet to the south, had the additional element OE læs, 'pasture', and indicates the pasture belonging to the village of Elswick.

Elterwater swan lake (ON elptr + vatn → Heltewatra c.1160). OE wæter has been substituted for the ON second element.

Elton Ella's *tūn* (OE Ella + tūn → Elleton 1246).

Eltonhead the hill by Ella's *tūn* (OE Ella + tūn + hēafod → Eltoneheued 1230). The name is a hill-name which contains an earlier settlement-name, Elton.

Entwistle river-fork frequented by ducks (OE ened + twisla → Hennetwisel 1212 → Ennetwysel 1276 → Entwissell 1311). The town is on a tongue of land between the Edgeworth Brook and a tributary. The first element has also been explained as OE henn, 'water-hen', and as a OE personal-name, Enna.

Escowbeck (R) the beck by the ash-tree hill (ON eski + hǫfuð + bekkr → Escouthebroc c.1225 → Escouthebec 1241 → Escow Beck 14th.c.). The first two elements constitute a hill-name which has been transferred later to the stream. The earliest form shows OE brōc, 'brook', but this was probably a slight anglicisation of an ON name.

Eskrigg ashtree ridge (ON eski + hryggr → Escrig 1202).

Esprick ashtree slope (ON eski + brekka → Eskebrec c.1210 → Esbric later-13th.c.).

Esthwaite eastern clearing (OE ēast + ON þveit → Estwyth 1539 → Easthwaite 1670). The name has influenced ESTHWAITE WATER, which in 1537 was Estwater and in 1539 the 'Mere of Hawkshed, Estwater'.

Euxton Æfic's *tūn* (OE Æfic + -es (possessive) + tūn → Euececeston 1187 → Eukeston 1243).

Everton pig *tūn* (OE eofor + tūn → Evretona 1094 (Latin) → Everton 1201). If correct, the first element has the sense of 'domestic pig' rather than 'wild boar'; but it may be the personal name, OE *Eofor.

Ewood wood on a stream (OE ēa + wudu). The name of two places:
(1) nr. Blackburn, on the River Darwen (Eywode 1246 → Ewode 1332);
(2) nr. Haslingden, EWOOD BRIDGE, by the River Irwell (Thewode 1269 → Ewode 1323).

Extwistle river confluence where the oxen graze (OE oxa, in the form exen (pl.) + twisla → Extwysle 1193). The village is at the junction of the rivers Swinden and Don.

Eyes, The land partly surrounded by water (OE ēg/ON ey – no early forms). The one-inch OS marks 'The Eyes' as an area between the River Mersey and the Manchester Ship Canal near Warrington. The word appears in other minor names – e.g. Thelwell Eye, Bretherton Eyes (Eys c.1250) and Eye Brook.

F

Facit the bright slope (OE fāg + sīde → Fagheside 13th.c.). The village stands on a western slope.

Failsworth ? enclosure made of hurdles (OE *fēgels + worð → Fayleswrthe 1212 → Failesworthe c.1200).

Fairfield This common, self-explanatory minor name occasionally becomes the name of a settlement through later building-development. Examples are FAIRFIELD near Droylesden, not marked on Yates' 1786 map but the site of a settlement established by the Moravians in 1783; FAIRFIELD, suburb of Warrington, named from Fairfield House, a hall erected among fields in the mid-18th. century; and FAIRFIELD, suburb of Liverpool.

Fairhaven new residential area of St. Anne's – self-explanatory.

Fairsnape beautiful pasture (ON fagr + dial. snape → Fayrsnape 1323). Since snape has the sense of 'poor pasture', it may be that 'fagr' was added as a distinguishing term to an existing name and has æsthetic reference. The name refers to a fell rising to 1,701 feet, and has been extended to the hamlets of HIGHER and LOWER FAIRSNAPE.

Falinge fallow land (OE fælging → Faleng 13th.c. → Falynge 1323).

Fallowfield newly ploughed land (OE falg + feld → Fallufeld 1317 → Falofeld 1417).

Farington tūn where ferns grow (OE fearn + tūn → Farinton 1149 → Farington 1246).

Farleton ? Farald's tūn (ON Faraldr + OE tūn → Fareltun DB → Farletone c.1195 → Farlton 1227).

Farnworth fern-enclosure (OE fearn + worþ). Name of two places:
(1) nr. Widnes (Farneword 1324 → Farneworth 1518);
(2) nr. Bolton (Farnewurd 1185 → Ferneworthe c.1200 → Farneworth 1278).

Fazakerley lēah near a border strip (OE fæs + æcer + lēah → Phasakyrlee c.1250 → Fasakerlegh 1277).

Fearnhead headland covered with ferns (OE fearn + hēafod → Ferneheued 1292).

Fence fenced-in area (OF defence, ME fence → Fence 1425). The name appears to refer to a late enclosure.

Feniscliffe marshy bank (OE fennig + clif → Faniscliff 1522). The village stands above the R. Darwen – compare *FENISCOWLES* further downstream.

Feniscowles hut in marshy land (OE fennig + ON skáli → Feinycholes 1276 → Feniscowles c.1300). The village stands above the R. Darwen – compare *FENISCLIFFE* further upstream.

Fiddler's Ferry The site of an ancient ferry across the Mersey and perhaps taking its name from a translation of Adam le Vieleur, who is supposed to have been the original grantee of the manor of Penketh in which the name occurs.

Field Plumpton see *PLUMPTON*.

Finsthwaite Finn's clearing (ON Finnr + þveit → Fynnesthwayt 1336).

Fishwick wīc where fish was sold (OE fisc + wīc → Fiscuic DB → Fiskwic 1202 → Fiswich 1203).

Fleetwood The town was founded by Sir Peter Hesketh-Fleetwood of Rossall in 1836 in the northern part of his estate and takes its name from its founder.

Flixton Flik's tūn (ODan. Flīk + -es (possessive) + tūn → Flixton 1177). The personal name is attested only in Danish sources and accords with other Danish elements in the place-names around Manchester (see introduction p.36).

Flookburgh fluke burh (OE flōc + burh → Flokeburg 1246 → Flokesburgh 1394). *Burh* probably here has the sense of 'market-town' and the name is probably post-Conquest. The first element could be the ON personal-name Flōki, but in any case the fact that flukes are caught at Flookburgh has undoubtedly influenced the name of this fishing-village.

Force waterfall (ON fors). This element common in minor names of the county, is seen in FORCE FORGE (Forse Forge 1668), FORCE MILL (Force Myln 1537) and FORCE BECK (R) (Fosse 1577).

Ford ford (OE ford → Forde 1323). The village is near a brook.

Formby the old býr (ON forn + býr → Fornebei DB → Formeby 1338). It has also been suggested that the first element may be the ON personal-name Forni.

Forton the tūn by the ford (OE ford + tūn → Fortune DB → Forton 1212). There were clearly two fords in the area, evidenced by Langwathforde c.1260 (ON langr + vað + OE ford, 'the long ford') and Scamwath c.1230 (ON skammr + vað, 'the short ford').

Foulney Island island of birds (OE fugol + ēg → Fowley 1537 → Foulney 1577). The island was a breeding-ground for birds. The change from Fouley to Foulney may be from comparison with nearby WALNEY ISLAND, although derivation from fūlan, a form of OE fūl, ,'foul', has also been suggested.

Foulridge ridge where foals graze (OE fōla + hrycg → Folric 1219 → Folrigge 1246). The reference may be to Pasture Hill, 786 feet high, to the west of the village; the original hill-name has become a settlement-name.

Foxholes foxes' burrows (OE fox-hol → Foxholes c.1200). The reference here is to a hamlet near Lancaster, but similar forms are found in minor names (e.g. Foxholes 1351 in Shevington).

Freckleton ? *tūn* by the dangerous pool (OE *frĕcel + welle + tūn → Frecheltun DB → Frekelton 1202). The etymology is doubtful, but the village stands on the old marsh road between Preston and Lytham on what was once dangerous marshland. *frĕcel welle would then have been itself a place-name.

Freshfield The site of the present village was originally called Church Mere. The township there was buried by sand in the period 1750-1850. It is said that the area was then made capable of cultivation by a Mr. Fresh, who laid top-soil over the sand, and when the land was used for further building, the new village was called Freshfield.

Fulwood the foul wood (OE fūl +

wudu → Fulwude 1228).

Furness Futh's headland (ON Fuð + -ar (possessive) → ON nes → Futh-pernessa c.1150 (Latin) → Furnesio c.1155 (Latin)). The name refers to the part of Lancashire north-west of Morecambe Bay and beyond the Cartmel peninsula, but originally it referred to a single headland. This headland may have been RAMPSIDE POINT, since opposite the point is *PEEL ISLAND*, originally called 'Fouldray', ON Fuðar ey. It is to be expected that the same first element would be transferred to the neighbouring headland, although fuð originally had the sense of 'island' and would have had to be regarded as a name in its own right before such a transference could take place. From there, it was transferred to refer to the whole region and the headland was renamed (cf. *AMOUNDER-NESS*). The district is divided into two parts, the southern part called LOW or PLAIN FURNESS (Low-furnes, 1546/Playne Furneys 1582) and the higher northern part called HIGH FURNESS (Heigh Furnes 1584).

Fylde, The plain (OE (ge)filde → Filde 1246), referring to the flat coastal plain between the Lune and Ribble and west of the Preston-Lancaster road. The word is a variant of feld, 'open country', which was used in contrast to wood and hill, and which later developed the sense of 'land for cultivation', equally applicable to this area.

G

Galgate the Galloway road (GALLOWAY + ON gata → Gawgett 1605 → Galgate 1786). The place takes its name from an ancient road running north through Kendal which is called Galwaithegate c.1190; the road is supposed to have been used by cattle-drovers from Galloway. Forms in '-w-' show a tendency to vocalize 'l' when it occurs between a vowel and a consonant, and should therefore be considered an alternative to, rather than an earlier form of, the '-l-' form.

Garstang ? a triangular plot of land with a pole on it (ON geiri + stǫng → Cherestanc DB → Gairstang c.1195). The reference may be to a boundary-mark, although ON stǫng can also mean 'pole, measure of length'. Other suggestions for the first element include ON geirr, 'spear', or Geirr, its use a personal-name.

Garston the great stone (OE grēat + stān → Gerstan 1094 → Grestan c.1155 → Garston c.1265). The reference may be to a boundary-mark, or to a prominent physical-feature, perhaps of the Mersey coast. The consistency of the '-stān' ending

in early records has led critics to prefer the above etymology to 'grazing-tūn' (OE gærs + tūn) which has been proposed. The change in position of '-r-' (cf. OE gærs → grass) and the change in the vowel before '-r-' (cf. person/parson) would be normal tendencies.

Garswood etymology doubtful (Grateswode 1367 → Gartiswode 1479), although the second element is clearly OE wudu, 'wood'.

Gateacre ? field where goats are kept (OE gāt + æcer – no early forms).

Gathurst *hyrst* where goats are kept (OE gāt + hyrst → Gatehurst 1547). The site, on the north bank of the R. Douglas, suggests a sense of 'bank' for the second element. OE geat, 'gate', has been suggested as an alternative derivation for the first element.

Gawthorpe Hall village where the cuckoo is found (ON gaukr + þorp → Gouthorp 1256 → Goukethorp 1324), the name of a hall on the south bank of the R. Calder. Gaukr is also used as a personal-name.

There is a GAWTHORPE in Yorkshire and it has been suggested that the name has been transferred from there.

Gawthwaite etymology doubtful (Golderswatt 1552), although the second element is clearly ON þveit 'clearing'. The hamlet is on an eastern slope near the head of a pass on the Lowick-Broughton road and the NCy dialect sense of 'the shelving part of a mountain side' may be dominant here.

Gerard's Bridge named from the local family of Gerard, a crossing-point on the Sankey Navigation.

Glasson the shining place (OE *glæsen → Glassene c.1265 → Glasson 1552). The main village today is on the Lune-estuary, near its junction with the R. Calder, where in 1787 a dock was constructed which later served a branch of the Lancaster canal. The hamlet of OLD GLASSON is further inland. It is unlikely that the name refers to a river. It has been suggested that the name may be a Celtic personal-name, in some elliptical form of tref Glassan, 'Glassan's village' (cf. WIGAN); Glassan is known to have been an Irish personal-name.

Glaze Brook (R) the blue/green stream (Brit. *glasto- → Glasebroc c.1195). OE brōc, 'stream', has been added later. The stream has given its name to GLAZEBROOK (Glas-broc 1227 (personal-n.)→ Glasebrok 1246), parish-name and settlement at a former railway-station by the river. The first element also appears in GLAZEBURY, on the GLAZE BROOK. The Celtic element may be

assumed to be the basis since this is a river name, but is difficult to distinguish from OE *glæs 'clear, bright, shining'. See also RIXTON.

Gleaston ? tūn on the brook called 'bright' (OE *glæs + tūn → Glasserton DB – Glestona 13th.c. (Latin)). The reference of *glæs, is doubtful. It may be the name of the brook on which the hamlet stands; it may suggest a sunny situation; it may refer to the 286-foot beacon-hill to the east and suggest a beacon-fire.

Glodwick etymology doubtful (Glodic c.1195 → Glothic 1212 → Glodwicke 1633).

Golborne the stream where the marsh marigolds grow (OE golde + burna → Goldeburn 1187 → Golburn 1259). The stream is probably the Millingford Brook on which the village stands.

Goldshaw Booth Goldgeofu's 'hut' (OE Goldgeofu + ODan. bōth, → Goldiauebothis 1324 → Goldiaue 1325 → Nethir-/Overgoldshagh 1464). The name has been much modified. In OE it was a woman's name and was, presumably, used with some habitational or topographical element. Later, as '-g-' was vocalised to '-i-' and the resulting '-di-' combination became modified to the final sound of modern 'judge', the second element of the personal-name was replaced by the more obviously meaningful 'shaw', OE sceaga, 'small wood', suggesting the woodland of the Pendle Chase. Finally, bōth, 'dairy farm', was added.

Goodber Common/Fell Goberth-

87

wayte 1588), apparently an OE personal-name *Gōdbeorg, or its ON equivalent, used with the ON þveit, 'clearing'. Earlier forms are required.

Goodshaw Booth Gōdgȳp 's wood (OE Gōdgȳp + sceaga → Godeshagh 1324), to which ODan. bōth has been added. The first element is a shortened form of what was a woman's name in OE'.

Goosnargh Gōsan's/Gusan's hill-pasture (OIr Gōsan/Gusan + ON erg →Gusansarghe DB→ Gosenarghe c.1212). It is probable that the personal-name indicates the Irish origin of its bearer – an Irishman or a Norwegian settling here after a period in Ireland.

Gore Brook the dirty stream (OE gor + brōc → Gorbroke c.1250).

Gorton the dirty tūn (OE gor + tūn → Gorton 1282). The first element may, however, be the river name, the GORE BROOK, which has the same derivation.

Goyt (R) stream, water-course (OE *gota – no early forms).

Grange-Over-Sands the grange above the sands of Morecambe Bay (Fr., ME grange → Grange 1491). The outlying farm to which the name refers belonged to Cartmel Priory. This later became the Grange Farm and this gave its name to the village as it developed as a coastal resort. Grange was the terminus of one of the routes across the sands of Morecambe Bay and was usually approached by coach across the sands in the mid-nineteenth century,

hence the final elements.

Grassendale the valley growing with grass (OE *gærsen + dæl → Gresynd-ale 13th.c.). The continuing significance of the first element is attested by the form 'Gresselond Dale' noted by VCH. The site is between the R. Mersey and the lower slopes of Woolton Hill at Allerton.

Great – For names prefaced by GREAT (other than that below), see under the second element.

Great Hill the great hill (OE grēat + hyll → Greithill 1527), referring to a hill over 1,200 feet high near Withnell.

Greaves grove (OE græfe→ Greues 1246), also a common element in minor names.

Greenacres A self-explanatory minor name. The modern suburb of Oldham developed after an act of 1807 permitted the enclosure of the common land called GREENACRES MOOR.

Green Ayre See AYRE.

Greenbank the green (i.e. grassy) slope (OE grēne + banca → Grenebanc c.1245). The form given is for GREENBANK near Lancaster, but this is a common minor name.

Greenhalgh the green hollow (OE grēne + holh), the name of two places:
(1) in the Fylde (Greneholf DB), a hamlet between low hills to east and west – see THISTLETON;
(2) a castle-ruin near Bonds (Grenolf 1347).

Greenodd the green (i.e. grassy) promontory (ON grœnn + oddi → Green Odd 1774). The promontory is formed by the confluence of the rivers Leven and Crake.

Greeta (R) the stony stream (ON grjót + á → Gretagila c.1215 → the Gretey 1577). The earliest form shows compounding with ON gil, 'ravine'.

Greetby Hill the stony *býr* (ON grjót + býr → Grittebi c.1190 → Greteby 1246).

Gressingham *hām/tūn* where there is grazing (OE *gærsing + tūn/hām → Ghersinctune DB → Gersingeham 1183 → Gressingham 1206). The earliest form shows *tūn*, perhaps the original form later replaced by *hām*, but more probably an error since *hām* does not remain a productive form into late OE. If *tūn* was the original, a more likely possibility as a second element to replace it is OE hamm, 'meadow, water-meadow', since the village is near the Lune, in a valley on a small stream.

Greystoneley *lēah* by the grey stone (OE græg + stān + lēah → Graystonlegh 1462).

Grimeford Village No early forms. Saxton's 1577 map gives Andertonford (see *ANDERTON*), suggesting that there was a ford over the R. Douglas here. Yates' 1786 map has Headless Cross, referring to a cross still surviving. The 1840 OS map has Grindford Farm. If the name is old, the ON personal name Grímr might be suspected, or perhaps OE *grendel, 'gravelly place',

to explain to 1840 form; but these are speculative.

Grimsargh Grim's hill-pasture (ON Grímr + erg → Grimesarge DB → Grimisarche c.1245 → Grimmisarghe pre-1262).

Grimshaw the wood where the spectre lurks (OE grima + sceaga → Grineschare 1265 → Grymeschawe 1284 → Grymshagh 1376). The possibility that the first element is ON Grímr, a personal name, has also been suggested, as has OE grim(m), 'dark, forbidding'.

Grizebeck the brook where the pigs are kept (ON griss + bekkr → Grisebek 13th.c.). The hamlet stands on a small stream.

Grizedale the valley where pigs are kept (ON griss + dalr), the name of two places:
(1) hamlet and brook north of Satterthwaite (Grysdale 1336), where the reference is to the valley north of Satterthwaite through which the beck flows; the valley forms a major division between the Coniston and Windermere fells and gives its name to the whole area of the GRIZEDALE FOREST.
(2) the R. GRIZEDALE, a tributary of the Tarnbrook (Grisedale 1314).

Gummer's How ? Gunnar's hill (ON Gunnar + haugr → no early forms), the name of a hill of 1,054 feet.

Glynn, The cleft (OE ginn). The reference originally was to a passage from the North Cliff, Blackpool, to the sea. The passage has been eroded, but the name was preserved in 'The Gynn Hotel' and was extended to apply to the surrounding area.

H

Habergham Eaves *hām* associated with 'the high hill' (OE h*ēah* + beorg + -*ing* + *hām* → Habringham 1242 → Habrigham 1258 → Habercham 1269). The high hill would seem to be nearby *HORELAW HILL*, and the first two elements may well have been an early name for that hill. EAVES, from OE efes, probably here in the sense of 'edge of a hill', has been added later (Abryngham Eves 1510). The name has been claimed as an -*ingahām* form, indicative of early settlement (see introduction p.46).

Hackensall Hakon's mound (ON Hákon + haugr → Hakunhou c.1190 → Haconshow c.1190 → Haconeshaw c.1190 → Hakinshal 1245). The name survives as part of the parish-name, *PREESALL* -WITH -HACKENSALL, and as a hall-name. It is not possible to determine the reference of the second element, which may be to a burial-ground, as often in NCy, or to a hill resembling such a mound. There are several small, round 50-foot hillocks in this flat area which could explain the name. See *PREESALL*.

Haggate entrance guarded by a wicket-gate (OE h*æ*c(c) + geat → Hackgate 1640). The gate probably gave access to a park or forest. Yates, in 1786, calls the place High Gate.

Haigh enclosure (OE haga → Hage 1194 → Haghe 1292); ON hagi, 'enclosed pasture', is also possible.

Haighton *tūn* on low-lying land by a river (OE halh + *tūn* → Halcton DB → Halheton 1283 → Halghton 1311). The parish, and its hamlets of HAIGHTON GREEN and HAIGHTON TOP, lie to the north of the Savick Brook.

Hale areas of low-lying land by a river (OE halh, in the form halas (pl.) → Halas 1094 → Hales 1094 → Hale 1201). The village stands on a low ridge by the R. Mersey; Hale Coast is a three-mile stretch of the Mersey shore.

Halebank the bank of *HALE* (HALE + ODan., ME banke → Halebonke c.1240), the northern slope of the ridge on which HALE stands.

Halewood wood belonging to the

village of *HALE* (HALE + OE wudu → Halewood c.1200).

Halliwell the holy well (OE hālig + wella → Haliwalle c.1200 → Haliwell 1246). Ekwall notes that a holy well is marked on the old OS maps. The earliest form shows a development from Mcn wælla.

Halsall low-lying land belonging to *Hæl (OE *Hæl + -es (possessive) + halh → Heleshale DB → Halsale 1212). The village is in the east of the parish, while westwards to the coast is the low land of Halsall Moss.

Halsnead half-part of a detached piece of ground (OE half + snǣd → Grewinton Halfsnede 12th.c. → Halsnade 1246). The earliest form shows that this detached piece of ground – now parkland – was owned by *CRONTON*, a village to the south-east. Some unvoicing of the final consonant is indicated by Halse net 1403 and Hallsnatt 1471/2.

Halton *tūn* in the bend of a river (OE halh + tūn → Haltune DB → Halhton 1401). The village stands on the R. Lune; the name probably refers to a sharp bend in the river 1¼ miles to the east which produces a sharp southward promontory.

Hambleton ? *tūn* by the winding river (OE *hamol + tūn → Hameltune DB). *hamol may refer to a flat-topped hill or a winding river, since its sense seems to be 'crooked, scarred, mutilated'. The name may refer to the winding course of the R. Wyre; it may, however, also refer to one of the flat-topped, 50-foot hillocks near the village.

Hameldon scarred hill (OE *hamol + dūn → Hameldon 1194), the name of two hills south-west of Burnley, distinguished as HAMELDON HILL, 1,305 feet, and GREAT HAMELDON, 1,343 feet. The meaning of the first element is uncertain; the sense of 'flat-topped hill' would not be inappropriate here, but 'bare, treeless' has also been suggested.

Hamer cliff (OE hamor/ON hamarr → Hamer 1572).

Hampsfield Hamr's fell (ON Hamr + fjall → Hamesfell c.1295 → Hampesfell 1537 → Hamfeldhall 1577 → Hampffield Fell 1786). The name refers primarily to the long fell, but has been transferred to the hall and village on its lower slopes. The confusion of the second element with OE feld, 'open country', but more specifically 'land for pasture or cultivation' and from ME 'an enclosed or fenced-in plot of land', may well have been aided by this transfer. The new form was then reapplied also to the fell.

Hapton *tūn* by a hill (OE hēap + tūn → Apton 1243 → Hapton 1246). The village stands in a valley at the foot of a 550-foot-high hill, while the parish continues its southerly rise to the two *HAMELDON* hills.

Harcles Hill Arnkell's hill (ON Arnkell + haugr → Arkilishou 1236), the name of a 1,216 foot hill, in which OE hyll, 'hill', has later been substituted for the ON second element.

91

Hardhorn store-house (OE hord-ærn → Hordern 1298). See *NEWTON*.

Hardshaw etymology doubtful (Haureteschagh 1339 → Hardeschawe 1391). The second element appears to be OE sceaga, 'copse'; OE heorot, 'hart, stag', may form the first element, but earlier forms are required.

Hare Appletree ? the grey appletree (OE hār + æppel + trēow → Herdappetire 1202 → Harapeltre 1322). The name clearly refers to a tree which served as a notable landmark. The earliest recorded form may be an error, although the occasional use of 'hard' in dialect in the sense of 'full-grown' has been noted. It has been suggested that, through use with words referring to boundary-marks, hār came to mean 'boundary'. The hamlet bearing this name stands at the foot of HARE APPLETREE FELL, at whose 1531-foot summit three parishes meet.

Haresfinch etymology doubtful and no certain early forms.

Harpurhey Harpour's enclosure (Harpour + OE hege → Harpourhey 1320). Ekwall suggests that the name may derive "from the eighty acres demised for life to William Harpour before 1322".

Harrock Hill hill where the grey oak-tree grows (OE hār + āc + hyll → Harakiskare c.1260 → Harrok Hyll 1501). The first form refers not to the hill but to low-lying land, ON kjarr, 'brushwood, marsh'. It has been suggested that, through use with words referring to boundary markers, hār came to mean 'boundary'. Here the hill, rising to a height of over 500 feet above the low land and mosses to the north, along the R. Yarrow, would be an outstanding landmark, presumably with an oak near its summit.

Harterbeck hart's stream (ON hjǫrtr, in the form hjartar (possessive) + bekkr → Hatherbecke 1576 → Harterbeck 1587), a stream-name which has also become a hamlet-name.

Hartley's Village This collection of workers' houses takes its name from William Hartley, who built them in 1888 for the workers at his jam factory.

Hartshead hart's hill (OE heorot + -es (possessive) + hēafod → Hertesheued 1200). The parish takes its name from the 925-foot HARTSHEAD PIKE (OE pīc, 'pointed hill, hill').

Harwood Either (1) the wood where hares are found; or (2) the grey wood (OE (1) hara; or (2) hār + wudu). It has been suggested that, through use with words referring to boundary-marks, hār came to mean 'boundary'. The name of two places:
(1) HARWOOD, north-east of Bolton (Harewode 1212);
(2) GREAT HARWOOD (majori Harewuda 1123 (Latin)/Harwode c.1300). The first part, GREAT, was added to distinguish the town from LITTLE HARWOOD (Little Harewud 1246/ Parua Harewode 1309) to the south-west. The latter is now a minor name.

Haskayne marsh (OWelsh hescenn →

Hasken 1329). The Celtic root has the sense 'rush', but 'marsh' is clearly indicated by the low-lying ground in which the hamlet stands. cf. *HESKIN*.

Haslingden the valley where hazel-trees grow (OE *hæslen + denu → Haselingedon 1242 → Haslingden 1296). The town lies in a valley surrounded by moors. To the west is HASLINGDEN GRANE (HASLINGDEN + ON grein, 'small valley forking off from another'), taking its name from the valley running west from HASLINGDEN. cf. Long Grain, to the south.

Haughton *tūn* by a *halh* (OE halh + tūn → Halghton 1307 → Haughton 1311). *halh* seems to have the meaning 'low-lying land by a river', the place being by the R. Tame.

Haulgh nook of land (OE halh → Halgh 1332).

Haverthwaite clearing where oats are grown (ON hafri + þveit → Haverthwayt 1336). The steep fells to the north-east and south-east of the village are still heavily wooded.

Hawcoat cottages on enclosed land (OE haga + cot + -u (pl.) → Hawcote c.1535).

Hawes This occurs in the names of two places;
(1) HAWES SIDE, district of *BLACKPOOL*, so-called because it marks a boundary of the former common of 1800 acres called Layton Hawes which was enclosed in 1769 (OE haga, in the sense of 'messuage, property' → Howes inter Lithum et Laton 13th.c.);
(2) HAWES WATER, 'narrow neck of land, pass through hills' (OE, ON hals). The lake lies in a valley enclosed by low but steep hills – compare the nearby name WATERSLACK. In 1246 the lake was called Arnolvesheued Dub (OE Earnwulf + -es (possessive) + hēafod + dubb), 'the pool by the hill belonging to Earnwulf' or, more probably, 'the pool near *ARNSIDE*.

Hawkshaw Lane hawk's wood (OE hafoc + sceaga → Hauekesheghe 1219 → Howkeshagh 1509), to which LANE, 'lane, narrow road' (OE lane) has been added.

Hawkshead The name of two places:
(1) hamlet one mile N of Caton, 'Haukr's hill' (ON Haukr + hofuð → Houkeshout c.1250 → Haukesheued c.1250), with the second element later being replaced by OE hēafod. The hamlet stands on high ground north of the R. Lune in a trough between two hill-tops;
(2) market-town in High Furness, 'Haukr's shieling' (ON Haukr + sætr → Houksete c.1200 → Haukesset c.1220 → Haukesheved 1336), with the second element later being replaced by OE hēafod. It has been suggested that the hill on which the present church stands was the site of the original enclosure; it may well have aided the later remodelling of the name.

Hawthornthwaite hawthorn clearing ON hag-þorn + þveit → Herthornthwaite 1206 → Haghthornthayt 1323).

Hawthwaite clearing on a hill (ON haugr + þveit → Hauthwayt e16th.c.). The present hamlet of LOWER HAWTHWAITE is at the top of a steep ridge.

Haydock place where barley is grown (Celt. *heidd + -āco → Hedoc 1169 → Heidoc 12th.c. → Haudok 1286).

Hazelrigg ridge where hazel-trees grow (ON hesli + hryggr → Hesilrig c.1200).

Healey the high *lēah* (OE hēah + lēah), the name of two places:
(1) near Manchester (Hayleg 1260 → Helay 13th.c.);
(2) near Rochdale (Helei 1215).

Heap Bridge hill (OE hēap → Hep 1226 → Hepe 1278).

Heapey rose-hedge (OE hēope + hege → Hepeie 1219). The hillside situation of the village makes OE hēap, 'hill', a possible alternative for the first element.

Heath Charnock ? stone (Brit. *carn- + -āco → Chernoc 1190 → Hetchernoch pre-1288 → Hethechernoce 1270). On the second element, see *CHARNOCK RICHARD*; the first element, added to distinguish the name from CHARNOCK RICHARD, is OE hǣð, 'tract of open, uncultivated ground', descriptive of the site.

Heathwaite clearing where hay was obtained (ON hey + þveit → Heittheuuot 1273).

Heaton *tūn* on high land (OE hēah + tūn), the name of four places:
(1) in Lonsdale (Hietun DB → Hetune c.1155). The village stands on rising ground in the low-lying district called HEATON-WITH-*OXCLIFFE*;
(2) northern suburb of Manchester (Heton c.1200);
(3) HEATON UNDER *HORWICH* (Heton 1227 → Heton under Horewich 1332);
(4) southern suburb of Manchester (Hetton 1196) whose areas are distinguished as HEATON NORRIS, granted to William le Norris by Albert Grelly the younger in the 12th.c.; HEATON *MERSEY*; HEATON CHAPEL; HEATON MOOR; HEATON *REDDISH*.

Helmshore cattle shelter on a steep slope (OE helm + *scor(a) → Hellshour 1510). The sense of the second element, 'shore of river, river-bank, steep slope', suits the site in several respects since the village stands on a tongue of land between the Irwell and Ogden rivers.

Henthorn copse of thorn-bushes where wild birds are found (OE henn + þyrne → Hennethyrn 1258 → Henethorn 1300). The second element has been later replaced by OE þorn, 'thorn-tree, hawthorn'.

Hermitage Green No early forms. The 1840 OS map marks the hamlet, by St. Oswald's Well, and a house, The Hermitage.

Hesketh course for horse-racing (ON hestr + skeið → Heschath 1288 → Heskayth 1298). Horse-racing was a popular pastime of the Scandinavians. The village is called

HESKETH BANK (OE banca, 'bank'), recalling the time before Ribble was made navigable to Preston in the mid-19th.c., when HESKETH was a shore village. See *BECCONSALL.*

Heskin area where rushes grow, marsh (OWelsh hescenn → Heskyn 1257). The hamlet is in low land by a brook to the east of Mawdesley Moss.

Hest land covered with brushwood (OE *hæst → Hest 1177). The village of HEST BANK (OE banca, 'bank') stands on the marshes beside Morecambe Bay.

Heyrod the high clearing (OE hēah + *rodu → Heyerode 1246). The hamlet is on the high west bank of the R. Medlock. Nearby names such as Hazelhurst and *HURST* attest the former wooded nature of the area.

Heysham *hām* in a wood (OE *hæs + hām → Hessam DB → Heseym 1094 → Hesham c.1191). Early forms reflect the modern local pronunciation 'Heessum', and it has been suggested that the name may be simply the dative plural of *hæs, *hæsum – cf. *LYTHAM.*

Heywood the high wood (OE hēah + wudu → Heghwode 1246).

Higham the high *hām* (OE hēah + hām → Hegham 1296). The village is on rising ground, at a height of 650-700 feet, north of the R. Calder, The land rises more sharply to the north, reaching 850 feet. See *WEST CLOSE BOOTH*

Highfield the high tract of land (OE hēah + feld → Heghfeld 1323 → Highfield 1653). The forms here cited are for the hamlets of FAR, MIDDLE and LOWER HIGHFIELD north of the R. Lune. The hamlets are on the flat top of a steep ridge, LOWER HIGHFIELD being just below the top of the ridge while FAR HIGHFIELD is on the high point of the ridge. The name, however, is frequent as a minor name – e.g. the HIGHFIELD district of Lancaster (Hefeld c.1225 → Heghefeld 1322).

Hightown the major town (High Town 1702). The name appears to be modern and self-explanatory.

Hilderstone ? Hildered's *tūn* (OE Hilderæd + -es (possessive) + tūn → Hildriston 1190 → Hildirston 1461). If this etymology is correct, the first element is the shortened form of an OE personal name; the first element may, however, also show some influence from OE *hyldre, 'an elder-tree'.

Hillam (at) the hills (OE hyll + -um (dative pl.) → Hillun DB). The hamlet is on low ground but near a number of small hills and itself on a slight ridge above the nearby marshland.

Hindburn (R) the hinds' stream (OE hind + burna → Hindeburne 1193).

Hindley wood where the hind is found (OE hind + lēah → Hindele 1212 → Hindeleye 1259). It has been pointed out that Horwich Forest lies to the north of the town; but that the land around the town is marshy and the sense of 'meadow' would also be appropriate for the second element.

Hoathwaite clearing in a hollow (ON hol + þveit → Holtwayt c.1276).

Hodder (R) pleasant stream (Celt. *hōð + *dubro- → Hodder 930).

Hoddlesden Hod's valley (OE Hod + -es (possessive) + denu → Hoddesdene 1296 → Hodelesdon 1324). The -l- is a late addition and has no etymological justification. The second element refers to the hollow among the hills in which the hamlet lies.

Hoghton *tūn* on a spur of land (OE hōh + tūn → Hoctonam c.1160 (Latin) → Hochton c.1200 → Hoghton c.1250). The spur appears to be the steep west bank of the R. Darwen.

Holcombe the hollow valley (OE hol + cumb → Holecumbam 1236 (Latin) → Holcoumbe 1296). The hamlet is at the foot of a steep slope on Harcles Hill; it gives its name to the HOLCOMBE BROOK.

Holcroft small field in a hollow (OE hol + croft → Holecroft 1246), surviving in HOLCROFT MOSS, low-lying land by the Glaze Brook.

Holebiggerah patch of land in a hollow where barley is grown (ON hol + bygg + vrá → Holbigwra 1332). The hamlet is by a small stream on a hillside. It has been suggested that a place called Bigwra was nearby, which would perhaps explain the addition of a distinguishing first element and might suggest that the sense was really 'the BIGWRA in a hollow'.

Holker marsh with hollows or depressions (ON holr + kjarr → Holkerre 1276). The name appears also in the parish-name of UPPER and LOWER HOLKER.

Hollingworth the holly enclosure (OE holegn + worð → Holyenworth 1278). The name is now that of a reservoir near Littleborough.

Hollins Green the ferry by the holly-trees (OE holegn + -as (pl) + fær → Le Fery del Holyns 1352 → Hollynfare 1556 → Hollyn grene 1577). The second element has been replaced by GREEN, 'village green', at a late stage of development, but HOLLINFARE is often given as an alternative form. The situation by the R. Mersey clearly indicates the sense of 'ferry' for the first element. HOLLIN(S) occurs in a number of other names (e.g. HOLLINS, HOLLINS LANE).

Holme island; piece of flat ground (ON *holmr*). The name of two places:
(1) HOLME ISLAND, an island off the coast near GRANGE (The Holme 1606);
(2) HOLME CHAPEL, a hamlet on the upper reaches of the R. Calder (Holme 1305). The chapel was replaced by the church of St. John in 1788.

Holmes higher dry ground among marshland (ON holmr → Holmes juxta Maram de Tarlton c.1210). The same element recurs in nearby HOLMESWOOD and is common in minor names.

Hoole shed, hovel (OE hulu → Hull 1204 → Hole 1212 → Hoole 1508), the name of two adjoining parishes, MUCH HOOLE (Magna Hole c.1235/Much Hole 1260) and LITTLE HOOLE (Parva Hole c.1220/Little Hol 1256).

Hope valley (OE hop → Hope 13th. c.).

Hopwood wood in a valley (OE hop + wudu → Hopwode 1278).

Horelaw the grey hill (OE hār + hlāw → Horlowheade 1578 → Horelaw 1598), the name of a 1,153 foot hill near Burnley. It has been suggested that by frequent use with words denoting boundary-marks, hār acquired the sense of 'boundary', and in hill-names the exact reference of 'grey' is often not obvious.

Hornby býr on a horn-shaped piece of land (ON horn + O Dan. bý → Hornebi DB → Horneby 1352). The village is in the tongue of land formed by the confluence of the rivers Lune and Wenning, which may be the reference. Alternatively, both village and castle are by a sharp bend in the R. Wenning. It has also been suggested that the first element may be the ON personal name, Horni, recorded only in EScand., and hence probably indicative of Danish settlement.

Horwich the grey wych-elms (OE hār + wice → Horewych 1254). The name clearly refers to the Forest of Horwich. It has been suggested that by frequent use with words referring to boundary-marks, hār may have acquired the sense of 'boundary'.

Hoscar the horse-marsh (ON hross/ OE hors + ON kjarr → Horsecarr 1344).

Hothersall etymology doubtful (Hudereshal 1199 → Hudresale pre-1240 → Hodersale c.1250). The second element is clearly OE *halh* in the sense of 'low-lying land by a river' or 'land in the bend of a river' since the district is the north bank of the R. Ribble near Ribchester where the river meanders. It has been suggested that the first element may be a personal name, OE *Huder. It may be noted that the site is 6 miles downstream from the junction of the R. *HODDER* with the Ribble, and the possibility of some formal influence from this river-name cannot be excluded. Forms in '-th-' are late; all early forms consistently have '-d-'.

Houghton Green tūn on a spur of land (OE hōh + tūn → Houton 1263 → Hoghton 1327). The hamlet is on a 50-foot spur in low land north of the R. Mersey. GREEN, 'village-green', is a later addition.

Hulme island, water meadow (ODan. *hulm*); the word is characteristic of areas of Danish settlement. The name of two places:
(1) near Winwick (Hulm 1246), in low land near the Sankey Brook and a tributary stream;
(2) suburb of Manchester (Hulm 1246), between the rivers Irwell, Medlock and Cornbrook; the early form, Overholm and Noranholm 1226, suggest ON *holmr*, but the 1246 form, and also Overhulm and Netherhulm 1324, have the distinctively ODan. element.

Hulton See *LITTLE HULTON*

Humphrey Head Hunfrith's headland (OE Hūnfri∂ + hēafod → Hunfridesheved 1199 → Unfrayhede 1537 → Oumfray head 1577 → Humphry Head 1786). The first element of the name has been confused with the later Christian name Humphrey.

Huncoat ? shed where honey is made and stored (OE hunig + cot → Hunnicot DB → Hunecote 1296) − i.e. a beekeeper's cottage. The alternative derivation is 'Hūna's cottage', taking the first element as the OE personal name Hūna.

Hundred End The name of a hamlet at a former station on the old Southport-Preston railway-line, so called because it is on the northwestern boundary of West Derby Hundred.

Hunger Hill the barren hill (OE hungor), a common hill-name throughout the country and occurring twice in Lancashire.

Huntroyde hunter's clearing (OE hunta + *rod → Huntrode 1412), the name of a demesne. The OE personal name *Hunta is also possible, but personal names are rarely combined with *rod.

Hunt's Cross etymology doubtful. The area seems to derive its name from a cross which stood in Oak Lane, Little Woolton. It has been suggested that the cross took its name from the fields beside the road leading to HUNT'S CROSS, which were called Hunt's Follies, after a group of buildings known as

Hunt's Folly.

Hurlston ? Heorla's *tūn* (OE *Heorla + tūn → Hirletun DB → Urltonam c.1190 (Latin) → Hurleton 1246). The forms are perhaps best reflected in HARLETON, the form of the name cited in *PnLa*. Forms such as Hurdilton 1468 appear late and suggest confusion with OE hyrdel, 'hurdle, wicker-work frame', which was the first element of Hurleston, Cheshire. Forms with '-s-' are late.

Hurst This common place-name element, OE *hyrst*, 'wooded eminence', is seen in two major place-names:
(1) near Ashton-under-Lyne, on high land to the north and west of the R. Medlock − the same element appears in nearby Hazelhurst and *LIMEHURST;*
(2) HURST GREEN, a hamlet on a hill north of the R. Ribble by the Dean Brook (Hurst c.1200), to which GREEN, 'village green' has later been added − the same element appears in nearby *STONYHURST.*

Hurstwood wooded hillock (OE hyrst + wudu → Hurstwode 1285). The hamlet is on the bank of the R. Brun.

Hutton *tūn* on a spur of land (OE hōh + tūn). The name of two places:
(1) near Preston (Huton 1180);
(2) OLD HUTTON, near Wennington (Hoton 1227).
See also *PRIEST HUTTON.*

Huyton *tūn* by a landing-place (OE hȳ∂ + tūn → Hitune DB → Hutona c.1193 (Latin) → Huton c.1245 → Huyton 1311). It is assumed that the landing-place must have been on the R. Alt and was therefore for flat-bottomed boats. The etymology is preferred because it permits the development of both '-i-' and '-u-' forms of the name from OE '-y-',

unlike OE hēah, 'high', which the modern pronounciation and the rise on which the church stands might suggest as a possible etymology. See *ROBY*.

I

Ickenthwaite clearing where squirrels are found (ON ikorni + þveit → Iccornewayt, Yccornethwaite c.1535).

Ightenhill ? furze hill (Welsh eithin + OE hyll → Ightenhill 1242). The parish takes its name from a 530 foot hill, now called Park Hill, on which the manor-house formerly stood.

Ince water-meadow (Pr Welsh *inis). The name of two villages:
(1) INCE BLUNDELL (Hinne DB → Ines 1212 → Ins Blundell 1332). To distinguish it from INCE (2), the name of the owners, the Blundell family, has been added. Other distinguishing references used in the past include Inis next Seftoun 1334 and Ines near Crosseby 1337;
(2) INCE-IN-*MAKERFIELD* (Ines 1202 → Ins in Makerfield 1332), also called in 1458 Ines next Wigan.

Inglewhite ? settlement of the

Angles in the bend of a stream (OE Engle + *wiht → Inglewhite 1662). The late form makes etymology doubtful, but the village is on a hill in the fork of two streams and in an area where, because of the large proportion of Scandinavian settlers, an Anglo-Saxon community might be distinctive. Alternatively, the first element could be a personal name.

Ingol Inga's valley (OE Inga + holh → Ingole 1200). The village later gave its name to INGOL HEAD (INGOL + OE hēafod → Ingalheide in Broghton 1490 → Ingolheide in Broghton 1496).

Inskip ? 'island' where wicker baskets are made (PrWelsh. *inis + OE cȳpe → Inscip DB). The village stands on a 67 foot rise with low ground on three sides. A 'cȳpe' was an osier-basket used for catching fish, but it is rare in place-names and this would be its only occurence as a final element. The name also appears in the form Inkeskip on maps of the sixteenth and eightcenth centuries. See *SOWERBY*.

Ireby *býr* of the Irish (ON Iri + býr → Irebi DB). The reference is either to an Irishman or to a Scandinavian who had come to England from Ireland (see introduction p.41).

Ireleth hill-slope of the Irish (ON Íri + hlið). The name occurs both in the village of IRELETH (Irlid 1190 → Ireleyth c.1200 → Irelith 1292) and as a distinguishing second part of *KIRKBY* IRELETH (Kirkeby Irelith 1278). On the meaning of the first element, see *IREBY*.

Irk (R) ? the angry little stream (OE irre + -uc (diminutive) → Irke 1322). The river is a tributary of the R. *IRWELL* and, although its etymology is obscure, it seems reasonable to suppose that the name derived from the first element of IRWELL, used as a simple rivername with the addition of a diminutive suffix.

Irlam *hām* on the R. *IRWELL* (IRWELL + OE hām → Urwilham c.1190 → Irwelham 1259). The name also occurs in IRLAMS O'TH' HEIGHT near Salford.

Irwell (R) the angry river (CE irre + wella → Urwil 1190 → Irewel c.1200 → Irwel 1246). The sense of irre may well be 'wandering, winding'. See *IRK*.

Ivah ? the edge of a hill (OE *yfer → Ivo 1520 → Ive 1528 → Ivah 1631). The hamlet is near the 647-foot IVAH GREAT HILL. Earlier forms are needed.

K

Kearsley *lēah* where the water-cress grows (OE cerse + lēah → Cherselawe 1187 → Kersleie c.1220). The earliest form shows a dialect-variation of cerse (compare the 'chester/caster' variation) and a second element based on OE hlǣw, 'mound'. The idea of 'water-cress' perhaps suggests more low-lying ground and makes derivation from lēah, in the sense of 'water-meadow', preferable; the parish is intersected by the R. Croal.

Keer (R) the dark river (Celt. *cero- → Kere 1262).

Kellamergh Kelgrim's hill-pasture (ON *Kelgrimr + erg → Kelfgrimeshereg 1202 → Kelgrimiserhe 1236).

Kellet slope on which there is a

spring (ON kelda + hliỏ → Chellet DB → Kellet 1194). The earliest form shows an anglicised form of the first element. It is the name of two villages, both in hilly country:
(1) OVER KELLET (Ovrekellet 1227);
(2) NETHER KELLET (Netherkellet 1299).

Kent (R) the holy river (Celt. *cunětio → Canc c.1200 → Kent 1208).

Kent's Bank the bank of the R. *KENT* (KENT + -s (possessive) + OE banca/ON banke/ME bank → Kentsbanke 1491).

Kenyon Einion's mound (OWelsh. *cruc Enion → Kenien 1212). The modern form probably arose from word-misdivision; viz. cruc Enion → cruc cenion. As often in Celtic, the personal name is the second element; the loss of the first element suggests either an elliptical form used by the Anglo-Saxons, who did not understand cruc, or the substitution of a more usual English word-order, with some word such as perhaps OE hlǣw, 'mound', replacing cruc – Cenion hlǣw – and this resulting phrase being shortened later. The name may refer to a former Bronze Age barrow known to have existed here.

Kersal *halh* where water-cress grows (OE cerse + halh → Kereshalam 1142 (Latin) → Kershala c.1175 (Latin) → Kersall c.1200). LOWER KERSAL is on the R. Irwell.

Kingsley the king's *lēah* (OE cyning + -es (possessive) + lēah → Kingesle 1246).

Kirkby *bỷr* where there is a church (ON kirkju-bỷr). The name of two villages:
(1) near Liverpool (Cherchebi DB → Karkebi 1176). The earliest form has an anglicised first element. The present church is dedicated to St. Chad, the seventh-century Anglo-Saxon saint Ceadda, and the ON form may replace an earlier OE name (e.g. cirice-tūn). Before 1766, when the modern church was built, Kirkby was a chapelry, but places with chapels of ease were not usually called KIRKBY and the name probably suggests a church independent of the Liverpool parish church at Walton;
(2) KIRKBY *IRELETH* (Kirkebi c.1195 → Kirkebi Irlid c.1190), so called in distinction to Kirkby Lonsdale, We. The dedication is again to an Anglo-Saxon saint, St. Cuthbert.

Kirkdale church valley (ON kirkja + dalr → Chirchedale DB → Kirkedale 1185). The main Liverpool-Ormskirk road goes through the valley, leading to Walton. The church to which the name refers is the parish church of Walton-on-the-Hill and the name indicates the route along which its parishioners journeyed. The earliest form has an anglicised first element.

Kirkham *hām* where there is a church (ON kirkja + heimr → Chicheham DB → Chercheham 1094 → Kyrkham 1094). There is much variation between ON and OE forms in the early period, including hybrids such as Kyrcham. Since the church is probably one of the three recorded in DB for Amounderness, it was probably of early foundation, and the name may well originally have been OE cyrice hām.

Kirkland grove of trees by a church (ON kirkja + lúndr → Kirkelund c.1230). The name probably refers to the church in the old village of *CHURCHTOWN*, although that at nearby Garstang is also possible.

Knott End-on-Sea the end of the hill/the end of the hamlet which is on the hill (OE cnotta/ON knǫttr + OE ende/ON endi → Hacunshou Cnote c.1265). The village is on the northern point of the estuary of the R. Wyre and the name presumably refers to the end of the coast. The earliest recorded form represents *HACKENSALL* KNOTT.

Knotty Ash A modern name, referring to a gnarled ash-tree which grew at the top of Thomas Lane in an open area of ground (? Ash 1700).

Knowle hillock (OE cnoll → Cnolle 1246). The form here given is for KNOWLE GREEN, but the element is frequent in minor names (e.g. KNOWL MOOR).

Knowley *lēah* on a hill (OE cnoll + lēah → Knolhale 1288). The earliest forms perhaps suggest OE *halh* as second element.

Knowsley Cynewulf's *lēah* (OE Cynewulf + -es (possessive) + lēah → Chenulueslei DB → Cnusleu c.1196 → Cnouseley 1229). Some confusion with OE cnoll, 'hillock', is perhaps shown in the 1540 form, Knollesley.

Knuzden etymology doubtful. The hamlet (Knousedene) gives its name to the KNUZDEN BROOK (Knuzdenbroke c.1208), the upper course of the R. Blackwater. OE denu, 'valley', appears to be the final element.

L

Laffak law-oak (ON lǫgr + OE āc → Lachok 1246 → Laghoc 1271). The name probably refers to an oak-tree which was the assembly-point for a district – the first element also means 'district administered under one law'; although a minor name, it is of local historical interest. The

form LAFFOG exists as a modern alternative. Compare nearby *BROAD OAK*.

Lamberhead Green boundary hill (OE land + gemǣre + hēafod → Londmerhede 1519). The hamlet is on higher land between Upholland

and Wigan. GREEN, 'village green', is a later addition. Compare nearby *ORRELL*.

Lancashire the administrative area whose principal town is *LANCAS-TER* (LANCASTER + OE scīr → Lancastre 1140 → Lancastreshire 14th.c.) For further details on the evolution of this administrative area, see introduction, pp. 17ff. The late-sixteenth and early-seventeenth century manuscripts of the Chester Mystery Plays suggest the co-existence of two forms of the name – Lancaster-shyre in the three most conservative manuscripts and Lank-eshier in the two 'modernising' manuscripts.

Lancaster the Roman fort on the R. *LUNE* (LUNE + OE ceaster → Loncastre DB → Lancastrum 1094 (Latin, copy) → Lancastre c.1140), the name of the county town. The town stands on a bluff in the bend of the R. Lune at a point at which the river is still tidal and navigable but fordable at low water. The remains of a third- or fourth-century Roman fort have been excavated, but there is no record of the Latin name for this fort. On the establishment of LANCASTER as the county town, see introduction. In DB there are two manors of LANCASTER, one as cited above and the other Chercaloncastre; in the second form, OE cirice or ON kirkja, 'church', has been added as a first element – see introduction. The name contains two points of linguistic interest. First, the 'caster' form of the second element may suggest Northumbrian influence but is also characteristic of areas of Norse influence. Second, in c.1540

Leland noted that the town was corruptly called Lancastre for Lune-castre; the formal divergence from the river-name is due to the short-ening and nasalisation of the vowel of the first element.

Langho the long *halh* (OE lang + halh → Langale 13th.c.). LANGHO is on a steep ridge south of the R. Ribble, while OLD LANGHO is lower and closer to the R. Ribble in a tongue of land formed to the east by the confluence of the rivers Ribble and Calder and to the west by the confluence of the Park Brook and R. Ribble. The sense of 'tongue of land between streams' would be appropriate for OLD LANGHO. Compare, however, *LONGRIDGE*, on the opposite side of the R. Ribble.

Langley the long *lēah* (OE lang + lēah → Langele 1246).

Langthwaite the long clearing (ON langr + þveit → Langethwayte c.1300).

Langtree tall tree (OE lang + trēow → Longetre c.1190 → Langetre 1206).

Larbreck clay slope (ON leirr + brekka → Lairbrec 1212). The hamlet stands on a 67 foot hill in the low ground south of the R. Wyre; the soil is clay.

Lathom (at) the barns (ON hlaða, in the form hlaðum (dative pl) → Latvne DB → Lathum 1196).

Lathwaite barn in or near a clearing (ON hlaða + þveit → Lathwayt 1320).

Launds, The woodland pasture (OF launde → Laund 1246).

Layton *tūn* by a stream (OE lād + tūn → Latun DB). LAYTON HAWES lay to the east of *BLACK-POOL,* cut off from it by the Spen Dyke which, until 1730, formed the outlet of the stream draining Marton Mere. Modern dialect lode has the sense of 'fenland drainage channel', and some such sense might well be appropriate here.

Lea Town clearing in a wood — see *lēah* (OE lēah → Lea DB); TOWN is a later addition. During the twelfth century the township was divided into two estates on either side of the Savick Brook. The modern hamlet is on the site of ENGLISH LEA (Engleshele 1201); the minor name, LEA HALL, is all that remains of FRENCH LEA (Le Franceis 1194).

Leagram ? mark indicating a road (ON leið + *grima → Lathegrim 1282 → the park commonly called Lathgryme alias Laygryme park 1594). ON leið, 'road', and *grima, 'a mark or blaze on a tree to indicate a boundary', are found only in this combination, and ON hlaða, 'barn', and OE lætt, 'lath, beam', are both possible first elements. It has also been suggested that the name is an inversion-compound of the Celtic type (cf. *KENYON*) with the ON personal name Grimr as second element. The name is part of the parish name of *BOWLAND-WITH-LEAGRAM* and is also seen in the minor name, LEAGRAM HALL, hence the reference in the 1594 example above.

Leck brook (ON lœkr → Lech DB →

Lecke 1212). The village takes its name from the LECK BECK on which it stands. The DB form suggests that OE *lece, 'brook', may be an alternative etymology.

Leece woodland clearings (OE lēah, in the form lēas (pl.) → Lies DB → Lees 1269). Compare *LEES*.

Lees woodland clearings (OE lēah, in the form lēas (pl.) → The Leese 1604). Compare *LEECE*.

Leigh meadow land — see *lēah* (OE lēah → Lecthe c.1265 → Legh 1276). The town stands on the northern edge of a large tract of mossland and the sense of 'meadow' may therefore be preferred to that of 'woodland glade'. Compare *EAST-LEIGH.*

Leighton Beck (R) herb-garden (OE lēac-tūn → Betheleghton 1246 → Lecton 1255). The stream takes its name from a settlement name, seen in the minor name, LEIGHTON HALL, to which has been added ON bekkr, 'stream'; the earliest form shows as first element either a variation of ON bekkr or OE bece, 'stream'.

Leven **(R)** etymology doubtful (Leuena c.1160 (Latin) → Leven 1196). It has been suggested that the name derives from a Celt. root *leib-, 'to drip' — either 'the slow-moving river' or 'the easily-flowing (i.e. swift) river'; either meaning would be appropriate to sections of the river. Welsh llyfn, 'smooth', exemplifies a modern development in Celtic.

Levenshulme Lēofwine's *holmr* (OE Lēofwine + -s (possessive) + ON holmr → Lewyneshulm 1246 → Levensholme 1332). The form of the second element today and in the 1246 form above shows the characteristically ODan. form, hulm; see introduction, p. 45.

Lever reed-bed (OE læfer). The name of three places:
(1) GREAT LEVER (Magna Leure 1285/Great Leure 1326);
(2) LITTLE LEVER (Parva Lefre 1212/Little Lethre 1221);
(3) DARCY LEVER (Darcye Lever 1590).
The name appears to refer to a variety of water-plants – rushes, reeds, irises. All three places are by the R. Croal – DARCY LEVER near its junction with the Bradshaw Brook and LITTLE LEVER near its junction with the R. Irwell – and the name may well have referred to water-plants growing on this river, or may even have been a name for the river. The Lever family of GREAT LEVER were ejected from their holdings and exiled in 1477. After being pardoned by Henry VII, they returned to DARCY LEVER, which takes its first element from the family-name of Sir Thomas D'Arcy who gained possession in c.1500.

Leyland fallow land (OE læge + land → Lailand DB). The village stands on low ground by the R. Lostock and the name perhaps suggests that this was pasture rather than arable land. The village gave its name to Lancashire's smallest hundred (Leylondshire 1410).

Lickle (R) etymology doubtful

(Licul 1140). ON hylr, 'pool', has been suggested as the second element, with ON lykkja, 'loop', or OE lyce, 'leech', as the first element, but this seems unlikely. A Celt. *liwcyl, 'bright' – 'narrow', has also been proposed.

Limehurst copse within the *LYME* (LYME + OE hyrst → Lymehirst 1379). Compare nearby *HURST* and Hazelhurst. Despite the modern form, the first element can not mean 'lime-tree', which in OE would be lind.

Linacre flax field (OE līn + æcer → Linacre 1212 → Lynaker pre-1290).

Lindal valley where lime-trees grow (ON lind + dalr → Lindale c.1220 → Lindal c.1225). The village stands in a valley through which run the road and rail routes from Ulverston to Barrow. Compare *LINDALE*.

Lindale valley where lime-trees grow (ON lind + dalr → Lindale 1246). The village stands at the southern end of the steep Newton Fell, with Hampsfield Fell to the south-west; north-west, the road follows the valley below Newton Fell to Newby Bridge. Lime-trees still grow there. Compare *LINDAL*.

Litherland land on a slope (ON hlið + -ar (possessive) + land → Liderlant DB → Litherlande 1202). What is today a northern extension of Liverpool covers the rising ground by the mouth of the R. Mersey. The place is also known as DOWNLITH-ERLAND (Dunlytherlond 1298) in distinction to UPLITHERLAND (Literland DB → Litherland 1212 → Vplithérland 1194). Compare the

105

first element with some early forms of the first element of *LIVERPOOL*. The survival of an ON inflectional ending here is further evidence of a comparatively large and influential group of Scandinavian settlers in this area.

Littleborough the little *burh* (OE lȳtel + burh → Littlebrough 1577). The earliest form is late – perhaps the name is late; the exact meaning of the second element is therefore doubtful.

Little – For names, other than those below, to which LITTLE has been added as a distinguishing prefix, see under the second part of the name.

Little Hulton *tūn* on a hill (OE hyll + tūn → Hilton 1200 → Hulton 1212). The town stands on the southern slopes of a hill. The prefix LITTLE distinguished it from OVER HULTON and MIDDLE HULTON on higher ground to the north-west; sixteenth-century records distinguish Overhilton 1521, Medyll Hilton 1552, Netherhilton 1521, and the three hamlets are clearly distinguished on Yates' 1786 map. Today, only LITTLE HULTON appears on the one-inch OS map, although HULTON PARK, park and former seat of the Hulton family, still survives.

Little Mitton *tūn* at the confluence of streams (OE (ge)mȳðe + tūn → Parva Mitton 1242 → Little Mutton 1283). The name now refers to a parish bordered by the confluence of the rivers Hodder and Ribble in the north and Calder and Ribble in the south. Great Mitton, (Mitune DB → Mangna Mitton 1241), from

which the place is distinguished by its prefix LITTLE, is a village on the north bank of the R. Ribble, in Yks.

Little Moss A self-explanatory village and parish name. A comparison with Ashton Moss, to the south, may be involved.

Liverpool ? pool with muddied water (OE lifer + pōl → Liuerpul c.1192). The name presents many problems, partly because LIVERPOOL, as a 'planted' town which was granted its charter in 1207 by King John, was not previously important and its name is not therefore recorded in early forms. A second difficulty is the meaning of the first element in the etymology proposed above and generally accepted; OE lifer means 'liver', but the sense here proposed is inferred partly from the OE adjective lifrig, ME livered, 'coagulated, clotted', and partly from the fact that several other places in England have LIVER- as their first element, apparently with reference to a stream. A third difficulty is the probability that this was the name of a tidal creek, later called The Pool (Le Pull in Liuerpoll 1317), which became the site of Liverpool's first dock and has now been filled up. But the fourth and major difficulty is the variety of forms in which the name appears in early records. Forms in '-th-', such as Litherpol c.1224, are frequent but are dismissed as late by Ekwall; they suggest ON hlíð + -ar (possessive), 'slope', which would not give very good sense as a first element combined with pōl, but which might suggest confusion with nearby *LITHERLAND*, which does have hlið as its first element, or the continuing influence of a Scandinavianised form of an OE element. Other early forms have '-e-', as in Leverepul 1229, which might suggest OE læfer, 'rush, reed, yellow iris' or 'reed-bed' (cf. *LEVER*); such an etymology would be possible, but some forms are not early, and forms in '-i-' appear too consistently in early records to suggest OE læfer as the original first element; '-e-' forms perhaps represent only a late attempt to give meaning to an unfamiliar form. It has, however, been pointed out that the spoonbill is also known as the lever; the seal of the city of LIVERPOOL bears a representation of the eagle, the emblem of St. John, but this bird was later confused both with a cormorant and with a spoonbill. The confusion with the spoonbill may have encouraged '-e-' forms of the name. The eagle-emblem has long been associated with the city's name and is the source of the mythical Liver Bird (to rhyme with 'either', not with 'liver'), a local explanation of the name. Other forms, such as Lurpoill 1343, attest the considerable and confusing variety of the city's name in the past.

Livesey well-watered land where there is a shelter (OE hlif + -es (possessive) + ēg → Liveseye 1227). Although this parish includes hilly land, LIVESEY HALL stood by the R. Darwen, and the names of nearby *FENISCLIFFE* and *FENISCOWLES* – the latter of very similar meaning to LIVESEY – attest the nature of the surrounding land.

Lonethwaite etymology doubtful (Lonethwayt 1537), although the second element is clearly ON þveit 'clearing'.

Longridge the long ridge (OE lang + hrycg → Longryge pre-1246). The village takes its name from LONGRIDGE FELL, a long and narrow ridge which rises to the north-east of the village to a height of 1,149 feet.

Longton the long *tūn* (OE lang + tūn → Longetuna c.1156 (Latin) → Longton' e-mid 13th.c.). The township is four miles long and one mile wide and straggles along the Liverpool-Preston road.

Lonsdale the valley of the R. *LUNE* (LUNE + -s (possessive) + ON dalr → Lanesdale DB → Lonsdall c.1153), the name of the most northerly of the Lancashire hundreds, and therefore added as a defining suffix to some place-names. The name was also used with topographic rather than administrative reference outside the county; see introduction, pp. 18-19.

Lostock etymology doubtful. The name occurs three times:
(1) river-name (Lostoc c.1200).
(2) west of Bolton, on the R. Croal (Lostok 1205);
(3) near Eccles, on Bent Lanes Brook (Lostoke 1322).
EPNE follows Ekwall's original suggestion of 'place where there is a pig-sty' (OE hlōse + stoc); the first element may have the wider sense of 'shed, shelter', and the second a range of meanings including 'outlying farmstead'. Such an etymology would explain the settlement-names but would leave the river-name as a formation from a settlement once on its banks. Ekwall later, and more

107

plausibly, suggested, however, that since both settlements are on streams, it is probable that the name was originally a river-name, probably of Celtic origin. He compares a Welsh llost, 'tail', and suggests a possible *llostog, 'beaver', making the modern name a shortened form of a Celtic name meaning 'beaver-stream'.

Loud (R) loud-sounding stream (OE hlūd → Lude 1246 → Loude c.1350), probably referring to the river's faster-flowing upper reaches.

Lower, Low – For names which have these defining prefixes, see entries under the second part of the name.

Lowick leafy hollow (ON lauf + vík → Lofwik 1202 → Lowyk 1246). Vík is not a common place-name element and examples are usually from places on the coast. Here, however, the reference appears to be to the valley of the R. Crake, which forms the eastern boundary of the parish and in which the church stands.

Lowton tūn on a hill (OE hlāw + tūn Lauton 1202). The village stands on slightly higher ground in marshland. The name appears also in LOWTON COMMON and LOWTON ST. MARY.

Ludderburn (R) the clear/pure stream (OE hlūttor + burna → Litterburne 1537 → Ludderburne 1619), which gives its name to HIGH and LOW LUDDERBURN.

Lumb pool (OE *lum(m) → Le Lome 1534). The form cited is for a place on a tributary of the R.

Irwell in Rossendale, but the element occurs also in minor names.

Lune (R) health-giving river (cf. Ir. slán; Loun 1094 → Loin c.1158 → Lon c.1182 → Loon 1190). The above etymology is speculative, particularly since no word corresponding to slán is found in the Celtic language used in the north-west, of which Welsh would be a surviving modern example. The etymology was a late suggestion by Ekwall to replace his *PNLa* proposal of derivation from Alone, the name of a Roman station (Celt. *Alaun- → *Alōn- → Welsh Alun; meaning unknown). Later research has suggested that Alone may not have been on the R. Lune; there are linguistic difficulties in such a derivation; and the existence of another R. Lune in Yks makes it unlikely that the name of the Lancashire river can be explained by postulating exceptional circumstances. In her unpublished thesis, Miss Smith quotes the oral opinion of Dr. Melville Richards, an authority on Celtic, that derivation from *Alon would nevertheless be preferable if the phonological difficulties could be satisfactorily explained, and that the river-name could be "from the personal name which corresponds to Welsh Alun."

Lunt small wood, grove (ON lundr). The name of two places:
(1) hamlet near Sefton (Lund 1251 → Lunt 1344);
(2) LUNT HEATH, near Widnes (Lund 1292).

Luzley lēah where there is a pigsty (OE hlōse + lēah → Luselegh 1246).

Lydiate swing-gate (OE hlid + geat → Leiate DB → Liddigate 1202 → Lidiate 1212). The gate would presumably be to prevent cattle from straying from pasture on to arable land. The initial sound of the second element develops as 'y-', uninfluenced by the plural-form or by ON gata, both of which would produce 'g-' – an interesting point in view of the number of ON names in the area; the 1202 form may suggest a 'g-' alternative, but the 'y-' form is consistently attested, though in a variety of spellings – e.g. Lidwate c.1270, Lydezate pre-1290, Lydihate 1340, Lydeyat 1369.

Lyme, Lyne Early records often distinguish parts of the Honour of Lancashire which lie outside the county, in Derbyshire, Lincolnshire, Leicestershire or Nottinghamshire, as 'extra limam', 'beyond the Lyme'. The word comes from Celt. *lemo-, 'elm-tree', but is used of a forest area; it has been suggested that the word may have acquired the sense of 'frontier'. It appears in Cheshire place-names in LYME and in the defining addition of NEWCASTLE-UNDER-LYME Staffordshire as well as less obviously in the second element of AUDLEM Cheshire, BURSLEM Staffordshire. In Lancashire it similarly provides the distinguishing addition in *ASHTON*-UNDER-LYNE, a translation of Latin 'infra limam', 'within the Lyme', necessary because of the other ASHTON's in the county. It is seen also in *LIMEHURST*. It is notable that this word for a major forest area is Celtic in origin (cf. *MAKERFIELD*). The local survival of the word in the area can be seen in early minor names such as Lyme in Salfordshire 1401.

Lytham (at) the slopes (OE hlið + -um (dative pl) → Lidun DB → Lythum c.1192). LYTHAM is on the estuary of the R. Ribble and the name probably refers to the area of sand-hills along the coast. See *ST. ANNES.*

Lythe slope (OE hliŏ/ON hliŏ → Lyeth 1588), referring to the situation of the hamlet on the western slope of the Tatham Fells.

M

Maghull *halh* where the may-weed grows (OE mægðe + halh Magele DB → Maghele 1190 → Maghall 1278 → Maghull 1398). The village is in low ground west of the R. Alt. It is possible that the form of the name has been influenced by OE hyll, 'hill', since the village is on the 50-foot contour; a potential development, never fulfilled, is shown in forms such as Mahale 1220 → Male 1501.

Makerfield ? open land by a wall or ruin (Celt. *mac̄er-, from Latin mac̄eries, 'wall' + OE feld → Macrefeld 1121 → Makerfeld 1243). The word is often used as a name for Newton Hundred in early records and survives today as a defining addition to certain common place-names within that area – *ASHTON*-IN-MAKERFIELD, *INCE*-IN-MAK-ERFIELD, *NEWTON*-IN-MAKER-FIELD. The first element may well preserve the name of an old Celtic district, and its survival might indicate a continuity of Celtic administration after the early Anglo-Saxon settlement (see introduction, p. 36). Feld is here probably used in the sense of 'district'. Some early forms suggest that the first element

was regarded as a possessive, perhaps even as a personal name, e.g. Makeresfeld 1204; while others show a loss of '-r-', e.g. Makefeld 1206. Compare *LYME*, *LYNE*.

Mallowdale valley where mallows grow (OE mealuwe + ON dalr → Malydall 1574). The hamlet is on rising ground by the R. Roeburn, and MALLOWDALE FELL is an extensive fell-district to the west of the river, reaching a height of 1,750 feet.

Manchester the fort at MAMUCION (Celt. MAMUCION + OE ceaster → Mamucio (Latin) → Mameceaster 923 → Mancestre 1310). The first element is Brit. *mammā, 'breast-shaped hill' to which has been added OE ceaster, developing in the 'ch-' form characteristic of south Lancashire. The form Mancunio, found in Latin records, is probably an error.

Mansriggs etymology doubtful (Manslarig 1520 → Mansriggs 1577). The second element is ON hryggr, 'ridge', referring to the fell-slope to the west of the Newland Beck. On the basis of the earliest form, ON manslagari/OE manslaga, 'murderer', has been suggested, but the forms are too late to be certain.

Markland Hill boundary road (OE mearc + lane → Marclan 1278).

Marsden valley where there is a boundary-mark (OE mercels + denu → Merkesden 1195 → Merclisden 1258 → Markesdene 1360 → Mersden 1435). The reference seems to be to the valley of the Pendle Water. The township was divided into GREAT MARSDEN (Great Mersden 1458/ Magna Mersden 1491) and LITTLE MARSDEN (Parua Merseden 1468), of which the latter village appears on the OS map. MARSDEN has been engulfed by the later settlement of *NELSON*.

Marshaw wood on marshy ground (OE mersc + sceaga → Marthesagh 1323 → Marcheshawe 1324 → Merschasheued (undated)). The above etymology would seem to suit the site beside the R. Wyre. In *PNLa* Ekwall proposed for first element OE mearð, 'marten, weasel', on the basis of the earliest form; Wyld more plausibly suggested OE merce, either as the adjective 'dark' or as noun 'boundary'. Whatever the origin of the first element, it has probably been influenced by OE mersc.

Martin Mere *tūn* by the lake (OE mere + *tūn* → Merreton DB → Merton Mere 1396), the name of the most famous of the Lancashire mosslands, now lost following the draining of the mere begun in 1692 by Thomas Fleetwood of Bank and continued later by the Hesketh and Scarisbrick estates. It is marked on all early maps, drew comments from travellers and influenced settlement- and naming-patterns in the area. Its influence is seen in such minor names in the area as MERE SIDE and MERE BROW. The mere gave its name to a settlement, mere-tun, from which the mere then re-derived its name, with the addition of MERE. See *MARTON MERE*. Attempts have been made by antiquarians to associate the mere with the lake of the Arthurian legends from which King Arthur gained and to which he returned his sword Excalibur, but such attempts have no basis; compare *WIGAN*.

Martinscroft Martin's field (Martin + -s (possessive) + OE croft → Martinescroft 1332).

Marton *tūn* by the lake (OE mere + *tūn* → Meretun DB → Mareton 1183). The lake of MARTON MERE still survives, but the hamlets of GREAT MARTON (Great Marton 1297) and LITTLE MARTON (Little Marton 1297) are now some distance away from it; both derive their first elements from the reference to the mossland, and have given their settlement-names to the lake, with the addition of MERE. The mere has influenced settlement- and naming-patterns in the area; its influence is seen in the minor name, MERE-SIDE, south-east of GREAT MARTON. Compare *MARTIN MERE*.

Mawdesley Maud's *lēah* (OE Maud + -s (possessive) + OE lēah → Madesle 1219 → Mowchisl' c.1250 → Moudesley 1269 → Maudesley 1368).

Mearley boundary-*lēah* (OE (ge) mǣre + lēah → Merlay 1241). There is no village. The township was once divided into GREAT MEARLEY (Magna Merlay 1102) and LITTLE MEARLEY (Parua Merley 1444). MEARLEY includes the area from Clitheroe to the ridge of of Pendle, at the foot of which stands MEARLEY HALL. Possibly the ridge formed the boundary suggested in the name.

Medlar the middle shieling (OE middel + ON erg → Midelarge 1215 → Middelerwe 1227 → Midelare c.1230).

Medlock (R) river that flows through meadows (OE mǣd + lacu → Medlak 1292 → Medeloke 1322 → Medlok c.1540).

Melishaw etymology doubtful (Melanshow (undated)).

Melling the people associated with Moll or Malla (OE Moll/Malla + -*ingas*). The name of two places:
(1) near Halsall (Melinge DB);
(2) in Lonsdale (Mellinge DB) – see *WRAYTON*;
The name is generally accepted as a folk-name of the -*ingas* type, indicative of early Anglo-Saxon settlement. The possibility that the two names indicate different groups of the same family has been suggested; the name is found elsewhere in areas of early settlement, e.g. Malling Kent, Sussex. See introduction, pp. 37-38.

Melior bare hill (PrWelsh *mǣ → Brit. *brigā → Malver c.1130 → Meluer c.1204 → Meller 1524). The reference is to the ridge, rising to 733

feet and dominating the Ribble valley to the north, on which the village stands.

Meols See *NORTH MEOLS*.

Mersey (R) boundary-river (OE (ge) mǣre + -s (possessive) + ēa → Mærse 1002 → Mersham DB (Latin) → Mersse c.1226). The river is the present boundary between Lancashire and Cheshire and may well have formed the boundary between Northumbria and Mercia after 600 (see introduction p. 27). It is notable that such a major river bears an OE rather than a Celt. name, a fact which perhaps reflects its particular importance for Anglo-Saxon settlement-patterns and administration.

Micklehead Green the great hill (OE mycel + hēafod → Myckleheade 1600); GREEN, 'village green', has been added later.

Middleton the middle *tūn* (OE middel + tūn). The name of two places:
(1) near Manchester (Middelton 1194), perhaps so called because it lies between Manchester and Rochdale;
(2) near Heysham (Middeltun DB), perhaps so called because it lies between Heysham and *OVERTON*, and particularly in distinction to the latter.
The name is frequent as a minor name, e.g. MYDDLETON HALL, east of Winwick, relic of the hamlet of MIDDLETON marked on Yates' 1786 map (Midelton 1212).

Midge Hall *halh* infested with gnats (OE mycg + halh → Miggehalgh 1390). The hamlet is in low-lying land west of the R. Lostock, bounded to the north by Farington Moss. The mossland was formerly much more extensive than today and the place must have been on the very edge of the moss. The second element has become confused with OE hall, 'hall'.

Milnrow row of houses by a mill (OE myln + rāw → Mylnerowe 1554 → Mylneraw 1577). In the thirteenth century the place was called Milnehuses.

Mitton See *LITTLE MITTON*.

Monton Mawa's *tūn* (OE Mawa + -n (possessive) + tūn → Mawinton c.1200 → Maunton 13th.c.).

Moor Park Originally Preston Moor, this area was acquired by the burgesses of Preston in 1253. It was enclosed in 1834 and developed as a public park in 1867 to provide work for those unemployed in the cotton famine.

Morecambe The town takes its name from the bay on which it stands. The bay seems to have been so called because Whitaker's *History of Manchester* of 1771 identified the Kent Sands with Ptolemy's Morikámbē. The name seems to be of Celtic origin, the first element cognate with OIr mór, már, and OWelsh maur, 'great', and the second element being Celt. *camas, 'bay'. This identification was accepted by West in his *Antiquities of Furness* of 1774 and seems to have then gained general acceptance. Yates' 1786 map marks 'Bay of Morecambe' but not the town, which was a development of the following century. By 1844

POULTON-LE-SANDS was an established sea-bathing resort. In that year the Morecambe Railway and Harbour Project was begun, and work on the new harbour led to a new area of development, away from Poulton, with which the name MORECAMBE was associated. Although the official name of the company was 'The Morecambe Bay Harbour and Railway Company', 'Bay' was gradually dropped from the title. A writer in 1870 suggested that the name was adopted because it was felt to be more suitable for a fashionable watering-place, but until that year the town was still officially called Poulton. That the name was in use as a minor name before its official adoption is suggested by an advertisement of 1821, quoted by Millward, for a cottage to let at Poulton-by-the-Sands called Morecambe Cottage.

Moss Bank ridge by mossland (OE mos/ON mosi + OE banca/ODan. banke → Mossebanke 17th.c.). The ridge rises to over 250 feet between the R. Sankey and a tributary, with Reed's Moss to the west, and lowlying land, whose character is attested by the minor name Carr Mill (ON kjarr, 'marsh') to the southeast.

Mossborough hill by mossland (OE mos + beorg → Mossebarrowe 1516). The hamlet stands on slightly higher ground than the surrounding mossland.

Mossley *lēah* by mossland (OE mos + lēah → Moselegh 1319). The reference would seem to be to the land in the valley of the R. Tame.

Moss Side edge of the mossland (OE mos + side → Mossyde 1530). The form here cited is for the suburb of Manchester, but the name is frequent in the county.

Moston *tūn* in or by mossland (OE mos + tūn → Moston 1195).

Much – For names with this defining prefix, see under the second part of the name.

Musbury mouse burrow (OE mūs + *burg → Musbiry 1311). It is difficult to distinguish the second element from OE *burh*, and 'old fort inhabited by mice' has also been proposed.

Myerscough boggy wood (ON mýrr + skógr → Merscho 1246 → Mirescogh 1323). The name refers to the low-lying district south of the R. Brock.

Mythop the middle 'hop', i.e. plot of enclosed land in marshes (ON miðr + OE hop → Midehope DB → Mithop 1212). The hamlet is on a slight rise in low-lying ground.

N

Nateby ? Nate's *býr* (ON Nate + býr → Nateby 1204). The first element is doubtful. ON nata, 'nettle', has also been suggested. The low-lying nature of the site would make OE *næt, 'wet, moist', plausible, but an ON first element is more probable. Wyld observes that the place is called Aschebi in DB.

Nelson The town takes its name from the Lord Nelson Inn round which it developed. The township was formerly Marsden (see *LITTLE MARSDEN*), but NELSON developed because of the location of the cotton industry there. The inn is not on Yates' 1786 map but is marked on a map of 1818. In 1864 a local board was formed for 'the district of NELSON'.

Netherton the lower *tūn* (OE neoðera + tūn → Netherton 1576). The hamlet is on low land near the R. Alt. The comparison may be with *THORNTON* to the west and also in distinction to *SEFTON* to the north. Compare also *HIGHTOWN*, some four miles away on the coast.

Nettleslack valley where nettles grow (OE netele + ON slakki → Nettlisclak 1264).

Newbigging the new building (OE nīwe + ME bigging → Newebigginge 1269). The name is common as a minor name; the example here is for the hamlet in Aldingham.

Newbold the new building (OE nīwe + bold → Neubolt c.1200).

Newburgh the new borough (OE nīwe + burh → Neweburgh 1431). As *VCH* notes, 'the name indicates that a borough had been formed.'

Newby Bridge the new bridge (New bridge 1577). The name seems to refer to the bridge at this point over the R. Leven. It is evidently late, being first recorded on Saxton's map, and appears as Newbybridge in 1659. Although NEWBY would normally suggest 'the new *bȳr*', in such a late name it is possible that '-by' is here a late addition or that the bridge was called after a local family (cf. *PENNY BRIDGE*).

Newchurch the new church (OE nīwe + cirice). The name of three places:
(1) in Goldshaw Booth, NEW-CHURCH-IN-*PENDLE* – the chapel was created in 1529;
(2) NEWCHURCH-IN-*ROSSEN-DALE* (Newchurch Rossindall 1590) – a chapel was built in 1511;
(3) NEWCHURCH-IN-*CULCHETH* (Newchurch 1577).

Newland newly cultivated land (OE nīwe + land → Neulande 1276). Land has the sense of 'strip of arable land in a common field', perhaps belonging to the nearby Ulverston or Plumpton. The first element possibly implies that the land had

been newly reclaimed from waste.

New Laund new woodland pasture (OE nīwe/ME new + OF launde → Newland 1462). NEW distinguishes the place from *OLD LAUND*.

Newsham (at) the new houses (OE nīwe + hūs + -um (dative pl.)), the name of two places:
(1) hamlet north of Preston (Neuhuse DB → Newesum 1246) – the earliest form does not have the dative pl. ending:
(2) NEWSHAM PARK, a park in Liverpool (Neusun 1196).
The loss of the second syllable through weak stress has led to the re-formation of final '-sum' as '-sham', perhaps influenced by OE *hām*.

Newton the new *tūn* (OE nīwe + tūn). The name of seven places:
(1) NEWTON-IN-*MAKERFIELD* (Neweton DB → Neuton Macreffeld 1257 → Neuton in Makerfeld 1318). The distinguishing addition here given is the earliest recorded, although today the place is also known as NEWTON-LE-WILLOWS, presumably 'the NEWTON by the willows' as in the same name in Yks., and in 1628 it is also defined as Newton in Wynwick;
(2) NEWTON-WITH-*SCALES*, in the parish of NEWTON-WITH-*CLIF-TON* (Neutune DB → Neuton 1242 → Neutonscales 1511);
(3) NEWTON in the parish of *HARDHORN*-WITH-*NEWTON* (Neuton 1298);
(4) near Whittington (Neutune DB → Neuton c.1207);
(5) HIGH and NETHER NEWTON (Neutun DB → Newton 1537);

(6) in Furness (Newtona c.1195 (Latin) → Neuton 1190);

(7) NEWTON HEATH, Manchester (Newton 1322).

Newtown A late name, self-explanatory, frequently given to developments of the nineteenth and twentieth centuries. NEWTOWN, Widnes, for example, was a suburb of houses hastily constructed for workers in the local alkali works in the mid-nineteenth century.

Nibthwaite clearing by the new 'booth' or dairy farm (ON nýr + buð + þveit → Thornebuthwait 1202 → Neubethayt 1246 → Neuburthwait 1336 → Nybthwayt 1537). The first element may have been influenced by ON/OE *hnipa, 'hill', dialect nip, 'the steep ascent of a road, hill'. HIGH NIBTHWAITE's situation on the high land south of Coniston would help this confusion. The earliest form shows the addition of a distinguishing first element, perhaps the ON personal name Þor, or ON þorn, 'hawthorn bush'.

Norbreck the northern slope or hill (ON norð + brekka → Norhicbiec 1241 → Northbreck 1267 → Norbreke 1543). The hamlet is on the northern slope of a small hill between Great and Little Bispham. Another hamlet of the same name is on the southern side of a 76-foot hill to the north of the significantly named *HILLAM*.

Norden the northern valley (OE norð + denu). The major name NORDEN refers to a place in a valley north-west of Rochdale; the name distinguishes it from *SUDDEN*, on the southern bank of the R. Roch. The name also appears as a minor name in NORDEN (Northdene 1400) and NORDEN BROOK (Northdenbroc 1348) in Great Harwood.

Norris The name of the family who lived at Speke Hall, Liverpool, which is seen in NORRIS BANK and NORRIS GREEN.

North Meols the sand-hill in the north (ON norð + melr → Otegrimele, Oringemele DB → Meoles 1113 → Normoles c.1194 → Northmelis 1203). This parish occupied the sandy strip between Martin Mere and the sea and was named in distinction to South Meols, which has not survived as a name, and to Argameols, which was destroyed by coastal erosion; it remained in distinction to South Hawes. See further *CHURCHTOWN* and *SOUTHPORT*. The DB form contains the ON personal name Auðgrimr/Oddgrimr as its first element.

Nuthurst nut-tree wood (OE hnutu + hyrst → Nuthurst 1322).

Nuttall the bare hill (OE hnott + hōh → Noteho 1256). The reference is to the spur of land to the west of the R. Irwell on which the hamlet stands. OE hnutu, 'nut', has also been suggested as the first element. The final element has been confused with OE *halh* which, in the sense of 'piece of land almost enclosed by a river', has some partial application to the site.

O

Oakenhead hill where oak-trees grow (OE ācen + hēafod → Akeneheved c.1240 → Okenheved 1305 → Okenheid wod 1507).

Ogden oaktree valley (OE āc + denu → Akeden 1246 → Okedene 1324). The forms here cited are for the village near Rochdale; the name referred to the valley of a headstream of the R. Beal, but HIGHER OGDEN is on a hillside. The same name is also applied to two brooks, one in Roughlee Booth and the other near Haslingden.

Oglet oaktree by a water-course (OE āc + lād → Ogelot pre-1275 → Oglot c.1300 → Oglet 1323). The above etymology is suggested by the site, on low ground near the R. Mersey, but OE hlot, 'portion, share', has also been suggested as the second element.

Oldham the old *holmr* (OE ald + ON holmr→ Aldholm c.1225 → Oldelum 1276 → Oldum 1327). The town developed on the southern slope of a sharp sandstone ridge, to which the second element refers. The meaning of 'old' here is not certain, but the sense of 'long or formerly used or occupied' has been proposed.

Old Laund Booth 'booth' or dairy farm in the old woodland pasture (OE ald/ME old + OF launde + ON bōth → Oldeland 1462). The name referred originally to a dairy farm and its pasture, and a sixteenth-century farmhouse of that name used to stand on a bank above the Pendle Water; it is now the name of a township. OLD distinguishes the place from *NEW LAUND*.

Old Swan A district of Liverpool named from an inn. Until 1824 the inn was called 'The Three Swans', but in that year it was renamed 'The Old Swan' to distinguish it from a newly-opened rival called 'The Swan'.

Openshaw unenclosed wood (OE open + sceaga → Opinschawe 1282). Open is not common in place-names.

Ordsall Ord's *halh* (OE Ord + -es (possessive) + halh → Ordeshala 1177 (Latin) → Ordeshal 1201 → Ordesall 1486). The first element is probably a shortened form of an OE compound name, such as Ordhēah.

The second element may mean 'nook' or indicate the low-lying nature of the area.

Orford the upper ford (OE ofer + ford → Orford 1332). The first element is confirmed by the form Overforthe 1465; ofer usually has the sense of 'bank, river-bank'. Ekwall notes that the Roman road from Warrington to Wigan crossed the Orford Brook at Longford Bridge.

Ormskirk Orm's church (ON Ormr + -es (possessive) + kirkja → Ormeschirche c.1190 → Ormeskierk 1203). The personal name is probably that of the founder, although it is co-incidental that in 1203 Ormskirk was held by one called Orm. Although not mentioned in DB, there was clearly a church here in the Anglo-Saxon period; the modern church stands prominently on a hill amid the low land. The name is ON, but the second element in early forms often shows OE cirice, 'church'.

Orrell hill where iron-ore is found (OE ōra + hyll). The name of two places:
(1) near Wigan (Horhill 1202 → Orhille 1206);
(2) near Litherland (Orhul 1299 → Orell 1347).

Ortner summer pasture belonging to *OVERTON* (OVERTON + ON erg → Overtonargh 1323 → Hortounargh 1324 → Ortner 1683). The name indicates that this was common land belonging to the township of OVERTON, six miles away, before the Norman Conquest.

Osbaldeston Osbald's *tūn* (OE Ōsbald + -es (possessive) + tūn → Ossebaldiston c.1200).

Osmotherley Asmund's hill (ON Ásmundr, in the form Asmundar (possessive) + OE hlāw → Asemunderlawe 1246 → Osmunderlawe c.1265 → Osmunderley 1539 → Easmotherlee 1558). The village lies on the lower slopes of the fells, but OSMOTHERLEY MOOR reaches a height of 1,000 feet. The modern form shows anglicisation of the ON personal name to Osmund, but the inflection attests the primacy of the ON form. At a late stage in the name's development, OE lēah has been substituted for OE hlāw.

Oswaldtwistle tongue of land belonging to Oswald (OE Ōswald + twisla → Oswaldthuisel 13th.c. → Osowoldestuisil c.1230). The OE possessive inflexion, -es, is seen in the c.1230 form. Two brooks meet at this point. Attempts to identify the 'Oswald' with King Oswald of Northumbria have no basis.

Otterspool otters' pool (OE oter + pōl → Oterpōl 1228). The form cited here is for a Liverpool suburb by the R. Mersey, but the name occurs elsewhere.

Outhwaite Ulf's clearing (ON Ulfr + þveit → Wlvetheit 1199 → Ulfthwaite 1201).

Out Rawcliffe See *RAWCLIFFE*.

Ovangle ? above a river-bend (OE ofan + angel → Ovangle 1476). This etymology is speculative because the first element cannot be satisfactorily explained. The earliest form is too late to indicate a possible origin, although the hamlet is on a slight rise by a wide bend in the R. Lune, which suits the etymology proposed. Since the name is late, OF angle, 'angle, corner', would be a possible source of the second element, leaving the first element still more obscure.

Overton *tūn* on a river bank (OE ofer + tūn → Oureton DB → Ouerton 1177). The village stands on the north bank of the R. Lune.

Over – For names which have this defining first element, see under the second part of the name.

Oxcliffe hill where oxen graze (OE ox + clif → Oxeneclif DB → Oxclive 1201 → Oxcliff 1327). See *HEATON*.

P

Paddington a modern name, invented by Robert Halton, who set up a soap factory here in 1820; the name is first recorded in 1844. Although influenced by London's Paddington, which means '*tūn* associated with Padda's people', the name could also be regarded as a blend of the names of nearby *PADGATE* and *WARRINGTON*.

Padgate marsh road (OE *pat(t)e + ON gata → Padgate 1669). The name originally referred to the Warrington-Bolton road; it became a parish name in 1838.

Padiham *hām* associated with Padda (OE Padd(a) + -ingahām → Padiham 1251 → Padingham 1294). The name is indicative of an early period of Anglo-Saxon settlement (see introduction p. 38).

Parbold building where pears grow (OE peru + bold → Iperbolt 1195 → Perebold 1202 → Parbold 1243).

Parlick pear-tree enclosure (OE pirige + loc → Pirloc 1228 → Perlak 1228).

Parr enclosure (OE *pearr(e) → Par 1246). The form cited is for the township which now forms part of St. Helens, but the name is found elsewhere, as in Parr near Tyldesley.

Peasfurlong piece of land where pease grows (OE pise + furlang → Pesefurlaing 1246).

Peel enclosure; small castle or tower (OF piel/ME pele). The name of two places:

(1) PEEL ISLAND (the Pyle of Foudray 1577). The island was originally called Fouldrey (Fotherey c.1327 → Foderaye 1537); the etymology of this form is doubtful, although the second element is clearly ON ey or OE ēg, 'island'. The 'peel' from which the island takes its present name was built by the monks of Furness Abbey in the fourteenth century to protect their harbour and provide a place of refuge in time of war;

(2) hamlet in The Fylde (Pile 1593). No trace of the structure remains, but there is a field-name, Hallstede (OE hall + stede, 'hallplace'), which may indicate the site.

Pemberton *bere-tūn* on a hill (Brit. *penno- + OE beretūn → Penberton 1201 → Pemberton 1212). OE penn, 'enclosure', has also been proposed for the first element.

Pendle hill (Brit. *penno- + OE hyll → Pennul 1258 → Pennehille 1296). The name refers to a distinctive hill of 1,831 feet. Brit. *penno- means 'hill' but was evidently not understood by the Anglo-Saxons, who accepted it as a meaningless name and added their own explanatory gloss, hyll, 'hill'. With the combination of the two elements, the further explanatory 'hill' was added to give PENDLE HILL. The hill name has been extended to the PENDLE CHASE, a former forest-area, and the PENDLE WATER, a river. The latter, in 1516 Penhull Water, is shown by Harrington in

1577 as The Piddle – the reapplication of a hill name to a river evidently aided formal confusion with a river-name found in other parts of the country.

Pendlebury *burh* on PENDLE HILL (Brit. *penno- + OE hyll + burh, in the form byrig (dative) → Penelbiri 1202). The first two elements evidently developed as a hill-name in the manner of *PENDLE* above, although this name is now lost, and the later fortification took its name from the hill.

Pendleton *tūn* by PENDLE HILL (PENDLE + OE tūn). The name of two places:

(1) on the western slope of *PENDLE HILL* (Peniltune DB);

(2) north-west of Salford, near *PENDLEBURY* (Penelton 1200 → Pendelton 1201), evidently referring to the same hill.

Penketh the high wood (Brit. *penno- + *cēto- → Penket 1243 → Penketh 1259).

Pennington *tūn* paying a penny rent (OE pening + tūn). The name of two villages:

(1) near Leigh (Pinington 1246 → Penyngton 1372);

(2) near Ulverston (Pennigetun DB → Peninton 1187 → Penyngton 1327).

Penny Bridge This bridge over the R. Crake, built in the late sixteenth century, takes its name from the Penny family of Crake Side who settled c.1587 by the old ford of the R. Crake called Tunwath, 'village ford' (OE tūn + ON vað), perhaps referring to the lost village of Egton.

Penwortham enclosed *hām* on a hill (Brit. *penno- + OE worð + hām → Peneverdant DB → Penuertham 1149). The reference is to the hill on which the village stands, perhaps called Pen by the Anglo-Saxons who did not understand the meaning of the Celtic word. The DB form shows a corruption of the name by a French scribe.

Pex Hill etymology doubtful (Peghteshull 13th.c. → Peythishull c.1310). The second element is clearly OE hyll, 'hill', referring to the 200-foot rise. The first element may be the possessive form of some OE personal name (e.g. Peohthelm), but OE *pēac, 'peak', + -es (possessive) cannot be excluded on available evidence. Local traditions which associate the name with pixies, or with a legendary Peg Pusey of Bold, a jilted lady who jumped or fell to her death from the hill, may be discounted.

Pickup Bank hill with a pointed summit (OE pīc + copp → Pycoppe 1296 → Pickope Bank 1595). The village stands on the western slope of a 1,200-foot hill; BANK, from OE banca, 'slope', was added later in the name's development. See *YATE*.

Picthall hill with pointed top (OE *pīced + ON haugr → Pickthowe 1609 → Pickthawe 1644). The second element has been replaced by OE halh at a very late stage in the name's development.

Piel Island See *PEEL*.

Pilkington *tūn* associated with Pīleca (OE Pīleca + -ingtūn → Pulkinton 1202 → Pilkinton 1212 → Pilkington 1246). The personal name is a diminutive of some compound name such as Pilheard. The name may be an -ingatūn form, perhaps indicative of early Anglo-Saxon settlement (see introduction p. 38).

Pilling place where there is a tidal creek (OE pyll + -ing). The name occurs as a river-name, now PILLING WATER (Pylin 1230) and a settlement name. It also appears in PILLING LANE, 'the road to PILLING'. It has also been suggested that the name is a diminutive of Welsh pyll, 'pool, creek'.

Pilsworth Pil's enclosure (OE *Pil + -es (possessive) + worð → Pylesworth 1243).

Pimbo etymology doubtful (Pymbogh 1339 → Pinbogh, Pynbowe, Pembowe 1323).

Platt footbridge (OF plat). The name of two places:
(1) on the Gore Brook (Plat 1292);
(2) PLATT BRIDGE (Platte c.1230 Plat Bridge 1599).

Pleasington *tūn* associated with Plēsa (OE Plēs(a) + -ingtūn → Plesigtuna 1196 (Latin) → Plesinton 1208 → Plesington 1241). The name may be an -ingatūn form, perhaps indicative of early Anglo-Saxon settlement (see introduction p. 38).

Plumpton plum-tree *tūn* (OE plūme + tūn → Plunton DB → Plumton c.1190 → Plumpton 1327). The forms here refer to the village of GREAT PLUMPTON, which was formerly also known as Fieldplumpton (*FYLDE* + PLUMPTON → Fildeplumpton 1323) to distinguish it from *WOOD PLUMPTON*, further east. The prefix GREAT distinguishes the village from the hamlet of LITTLE PLUMPTON below it (Little/le Graunte Fildeplumpton 1323).

Ponthalgh etymology doubtful (Poutehalt, Poutehale 1288 → Pontawghe 1536). The first element has been modified, perhaps by confusion with OF pont, 'bridge'; the second element seems to be OE *hālh.*

Poulton *tūn* by a pool (OE pōl + tūn). The name of two places and the former name of *MORECAMBE:*
(1) POULTON-LE-*FYLDE* (Poltun DB). LE FYLDE was added to distinguish the place from (2). The first element probably refers to the *SKIPPOOL;*
(2) POULTON-WITH-FEARN-*HEAD* (Poltonam 1094 (Latin)).
(3) POULTON-LE-SANDS, the former name of *MORECAMBE* (Poltune DB);

Preesall hill covered with brushwood. The meaning of the name is clear, since the village stands on a 100 foot hill at the mouth of the R. Wyre. The first element is Celtic – Welsh pres, 'brushwood' – to which an OE second element has been added; the first element was obviously treated as a meaningless name (compare *PENDLE*) to which a descriptive OE word was added. Perhaps some distinction from *PREESE*, further south, was also intended. But there are several forms of equal antiquity from which the name may have arisen:
(1) OE hēafod (Pressouede DB →

Preshoued c.1190);
(2) OE *ofer (Pressoure 1094 → Preshouere c.1190);
(3) OE hōh (Preshou c.1190) – all of which would have the same general sense of 'hill', although OE ofer, 'shore', may also be a factor in (2). The hill may have had a variety of early names, or confusion may have occurred as the form of the second element changed under weakened stress. The name was subsequently reformed by substituting OE *halh* as second element. See *HACK-INSALL*.

Preese area covered with brushwood (Welsh pres → Pres DB → Prees c.1200). Compare *PREESALL*.

Prescot the priests' cottage (OE prēost + cot → Prestecota 1178 (Latin) → Prescote 1440). Cot may here have the sense of 'parsonage'. It has been suggested that the name indicates the portion of Whiston which was separated as an endowment for the church at *ECCLESTON* nearby. The reference to 'Churchleigh, now called Prestecote' in an assize roll of Richard II perhaps confirms this suggestion and may indicate an alternative or earlier name for the place.

Prestolee *lēah* belonging to PREST-ALL (PRESTALL + OE lēah → Prestawe alias Prestall Lee 1618). Prestall (OE prēost + hall, 'priests' hall') is in nearby Farnworth.

Preston priests' *tūn* (OE prēost + tūn → Prestvne DB), presumably originally an endowment to support a religious house which was not in the immediate area.

Prestwich priests' *wīc* (OE prēost + wīc → Prestwich 1194), perhaps a rectory, but equally probably a farm and equivalent to *PRESTON.*

Priest Hutton *tūn* on a spur of land (OE hōh + tūn → Hotune DB).

PRIEST (OE prēost, 'priest' → Presthotone 1307) was added to distinguish the place from Hutton Roof, We, and indicates that the manor was owned by the rector of Wharton.

Q

Quarlton mill hill (OE cweorn + + dūn → Querendon 1246 → Quarnton 1587 → Quarton 1587). Weakening of the ending has led to confusion with OE *tūn.* Cweorn, 'millstone', is used to refer to any kind of mill, and here may suggest a windmill; but it has also been suggested that millstones may have been found here.

Quernmore moor where millstones were found (OE cweorn + mōr → Quernemor 1228). Cweorn, 'millstone', is used also to refer to any kind of mill, and the meaning here might be 'moor where there is a water-mill'. The modern pronunciation, 'Quormer', shows the persistence of a rounded vowel after 'w'.

R

Radcliffe the red cliff (OE r ēad + clif → Radecliue DB). The name refers to the steep northern bank of the R. Roch.

Rainford ? the ford by a boundary strip (ON reinn + OE ford → Raineford 1198). The reference seems to be to the point at which the road through the mosslands which surround the village crossed the Sankey Brook. Lenney compares the minor Rainford name Rayndene c.1300. Ekwall prefers to derive the first element from the OE personal name Regna, 'the ford owned by Regna or which gave access to Regna's lands', while ON *raun, 'the rowan tree', has also been suggested. The first element is probably identical with that in *RAINHILL*, on a hill about five miles south of RAINFORD.

Rainhill ? the hill where there is a boundary strip (ON reinn + OE hyll → Reynhull 1246). The village is on the northern side of a sandstone ridge. The first element is probably identical with that in *RAINFORD* and Ekwall prefers derivation from the OE personal name Regna. Nearby is

RAINHILL STOOPS (1786), in which ON staup, 'steep declivity, precipice' has been added to the name.

Rampside the headland in the shape of a ram's head (OE ramm + -es (possessive) + h ēafod → Rameshede 1292 → Ramsyde 1539). The reference is to the 89-foot-high hill by the coast, at the foot of which the hamlet stands and which gives its name also to the RAMPSIDE SANDS. The second element has, with phonetic modification and an association of the name with the hamlet on the coast rather than the headland, been confused with OE' side, 'hill-side; land extending alongside a river or lake'.

Ramsbottom (Romesbothum 1324). Two etymologies are equally possible since the form is too late to be certain of its basis:
(1) the ram's valley (OE ramm + -es (possessive) + botm);
(2) valley where the wild garlic grows (OE hramsa + botm). The town occupies the narrow valley of the R. Irwell. Ekwall's further proposal that the first element is a personal name is less probable.

Ramsgreave the ram's grove (OE ramm + -es (possessive) + græfe → Romesgreve 1296). The name is a parish-name and is seen also in TOP OF RAMSGREAVE, the name of the 727-foot-high hill which is the highest point of the parish.

Raven Meols Hrafn's sandhill (ON Hrafn + melr → Mele DB → Molas 1094 (Latin) → Ravenesmeles c.1192). The place is on the sandy ground near *FORMBY*.

Rawcliffe the red hill (ON rauðr + klif → Rodeclif DB → Outroutheclif 1324 → Roucliffe 1399 → Outrauclif 1443). The township of RAW-CLIFFE extends along the mosslands to the north of the R. Wyre. The name may refer to the 50-foot-high ridge that rises from RAWCLIFFE MOSS, or to the small 50-foot-high hill beside the river on which stands the hamlet of OUT RAWCLIFFE (i.e. the place on the outskirts of RAWCLIFFE — OE ūt). The former seems more probable. Ekwall records an earlier MIDDLE and UPPER RAWCLIFFE (Uprouclelive 1246), the latter seen in the parish-name of UPPER RAWCLIFFE WITH *TARN-ACRE*. The DB form seems to show some influence of OE rēad.

Rawlinson's Nab the knoll (ON nabbi) belonging to the Rawlinson family who lived at Low Graythwaite House, Saltherthwaite.

Rawtenstall the farmstead on rough ground (OE rūh + *tūn-stall → Routonstall 1324). The town lies in the upper Irwell valley. It is listed as a cattle-farm in 1324 and it has been suggested that *tūn-stall may here show a specific sense of 'buildings occupied when cattle were pastured on high ground'. Ekwall prefers to derive the name from ME routand (present participle), 'roaring' + OE stall, 'pool'.

Read headland of the roe (OE ræge + hēafod → Revet 1202 → Reved 1246 → Reede 1528). The headland is rising ground between the Sabden Brook and the R. Calder which meet to the west of READ PARK, site of the former home of the Nowell family.

Reddish the ditch where the reeds grow (OE hrēod + dīc → Rediche 1212). It has been suggested that the name refers to the Old Nico Ditch which formed the northern boundary of the township.

Redvales halh belonging to *Redgifu (OE *Redgifu + halh → Rediveshale 1185 → Redyval 1296). The land lies between the rivers Irwell and Roch. Understandably, with phonetic change the second element has become confused with OF val, ME vale, 'vale, wide valley'.

Reedley lēah where reeds grow (OE hrēod + lēah → Redelegh Halowez 1464). The hamlet of REEDLEY stands on rising ground to the east of the Pendle Water; the form given above is seen in the parish-name, REEDLEY HALLOWS (OE halh in plural form halas), 'the halas belonging to REEDLEY'; Ekwall suggests that halas here means 'water-meadows', but halh can refer to a detached part of a parish and the sense may have been 'that part of REEDLEY parish which is separated from REEDLEY village by the Pendle Water'. The development of

125

halas has clearly been influenced by 'hallows' (OE (ge)halgas, 'saints'). Alternatively, halh may suggest 'land between two streams' – i.e. The Pendle Water and the R. Calder. OE lēah in this name seems to have the sense of 'meadow' and refer to the land immediately beside the river.

Ribble (R) ? the tearing or rushing river (OE *ripel → Rippel c.710 → Ribbel c.930). The Roman name for *RIBCHESTER*, Bremetonnacum, probably contains the Celtic name for the river, *Bremetona, 'the roaring river'. If this was the Celtic name for the river, the modern name is almost certainly of OE origin, but the suggested etymology is extremely doubtful. DB records the name as Ripam (Latin), showing confusion with Latin ripa, 'bank'. The area in the river-valley is RIBBLESDALE (Riblisdale pre-1246).

Ribbleton *tūn* on the R. *RIBBLE* (RIBBLE + tūn → Ribleton 1201), on the R. Ribble east of Preston.

Ribby *bўr* on a ridge (ON hryggr + bўr → Rigbi DB). The village is on the northern slope of a hill. See *WREA*.

Ribchester the Roman fort on the R. *RIBBLE* (RIBBLE + OE ceaster → Ribelcastre DB → Ribbeceastre 1202 → Ribchester 1420). The Roman fort, built in wood in the first century A.D. and reconstructed in stone in the second, was called Bremetonnacum. The fort was abandoned in the fourth century and the site renamed by the Anglo-Saxons from the river on which it stands. The DB form shows the

'-caster' ending characteristic of north Lancashire, the form often held to be Northumbrian but found only in areas of ON influence; but the modern form has developed as '-chester', characteristic of south Lancashire.

Rishton *tūn* where rushes grow (OE risc + tūn → Riston c.1204 → Rissheton 1322). A number of early forms show the '-u-' from OE Anglian rysc; e.g. Ruston 1300, Russhton 1332.

Risley *lēah* where brushwood grows (OE hrīs + lēah → Ryselegh 1284 → Risselley 1285). The name is recorded on the one-inch OS map in RISLEY MOSS, an area of moss-land near the R. Mersey north-east of Warrington. The character of the site, and the fact that it lies outside the woodland belt of medieval Lancashire suggest that the second element has the sense of 'piece of open land'.

Rivington The place-name refers to the 1,191-foot RIVINGTON PIKE at the foot of whose slope the village stands. Originally, this hill was 'the rough or rugged place' (OE hrēof + -ing → Rovyng 1325 → Rivenpike c.1540), the earliest form showing the '-o-' development of the North-west Midland area; to this has added PIKE, from OE pīc, 'hill'. On his map of 1577 Saxton calls it Rivenpike Hill. The village contains this name and therefore means '*tūn* by the hill called RIVING' (RIVING + OE tūn → Rowinton 1202 → Revington 1202). The village has later given its name to the hill, 'hill by or belonging to RIVINGTON'.

Rixton *tūn* where rushes grow (OE risc + tūn → Rixton 1201 → Riston 1246). The name is seen in the parish-name of RIXTON-WITH-GLAZEBROOK and in RIXTON MOSS which lie beside the R. Mersey. The etymology above is that proposed by Wyld and suits the nature of the site. Ekwall prefers to regard the first element as an OE personal name, with possessive inflection − Rīces or Rīcsiges. See *GLAZEBROOK*.

Roa Island etymology doubtful (the Roa 1577).

Roanhead the hill with the thicket (ME rone + OE hëafod → Ronheved 1338 → Ronehede 1539).

Roby *býr* situated near a boundary-mark (ON rá + bý́r → Rabil DB → Rabi 1185 → Roby c.1210). The village is on the Childwall border. The DB form seems to show some confusion of the second element with OE hyll, 'hill'. The name appears also in the minor name, ROBY MILL, near Dalton.

Roch (R) Two quite different etymologies have been proposed for the name (Rached 13th.c. → Rache 13th.c.): (1) Celt. *rac- + *cēto-, 'the district opposite the forest', presumably referring to the Forest of Rossendale which lay to the north; (2) a back-formation from *ROCHDALE,* whose first element is OE ræced, a by-form of reced, 'house, hall'.

Rochdale either '*hām* on the R. ROCH' or '*hām* by a hall' (ROCH/OE reced, ræced + hām → Recedham DB → Rachetham c.1193 → Rache-

dal c.1194 → Rochedale 1246). The word reced is not found in any other place-name, but *hām* is used with old place-names and river-names. Because of the identity of the river-name and the first element of ROCHDALE, the second element has later been replaced by ON dalr, 'valley'. The resulting syllabic misdivision of 'Racheddale' has perhaps aided the loss of '-d-' in the river-name.

Roddlesworth Hroðwulf's enclosure (OE Hröðwulf + -es (possessive) + worð → Rodtholfeswrtha c.1160 (Latin) → Rotholueswurth 1246 → Rothelisworthe 1283 → Roddlesworth 1559).

Roeburn (R) stream of the female roe-deer (OE rǣge + burna → Reburndale 1285 → Reborn 1292 → Rheburne, Roburn 1577). The '-e-' forms represent the regular development of OE ǣ; the later '-o-' form shows the substitution of OE rā, 'roe', for the first element. The earliest form shows the addition of ON dalr, 'valley', as in ROEBURN DALE, 'the valley of the R. ROEBURN', comprehending the wide tract of hilly country on either side of the river (cf. Rebrundale 1301, Rebournedale 1363).

Rooden hill on which a cross stands (OE rōd + dūn → Roden 1340).

Roose moor, heath (OWelsh ros → Rosse DB → Roos 1336). This suburb of Barrow-in-Furness lies in a valley. The name recurs in nearby ROOSECOTE, 'the cottage near ROOSE' (ROOSE + OE cot → Rusecote 1509), which in turn gives its name to ROOSECOTE SANDS and ROOSECOTE MOSS; and in the minor stream-name, the ROOSE BECK (Rosbech 1227 → Rosebec 1269), where the second element, OE bece, 'stream', was apparently replaced by ON bekkr, 'stream'. Ros survives in the dialect word ross, 'marsh', and the low-lying nature of the site here may perhaps indicate that sense.

Roseacre the field where there is a cairn or heap of stones (ON hreysi + akr → Rasak' 1249 → Raysacre 1283 → Roseacr' 1526). The name may refer to the same feature suggested in the name of *WHARLES*, about a mile away to the south-east. Wainwright has drawn attention to five instances of the field-name Wheel Meadow in the neighbouring township of Newton-with-Scales.

Rossall *halh* where horses graze (ON hross + OE halh → Rushale DB → Rossall 1212). The place is on the coastal side of the peninsula formed by the lower waters and estuary of the R. Wyre; the land is low-lying. The second element could therefore have one of a number of senses – 'low-lying land', 'tongue of land between two areas of water', and perhaps even 'nook of land'. The relationship of the first element to the second is debatable; it may be that horses were bred or raced here, since horse-racing was a popular pastime of the Scandinavians (cf. *HESKETH*). The earliest form suggests OE rysc, 'rush'. The marshy nature of the area is suggested by minor names on Yates' 1786 map – Carr Houses (ON kjarr, 'marsh') and Fenny (OE fennig, 'marshy') – which perhaps give some point to a possible confusion with risc. The name is seen today in ROSSALL POINT and in the public school, ROSSALL SCHOOL.

Rossendale? the valley in the moors (OWelsh ros + *-inn/*-enn (diminutive) + OE dæl → Rocendal 1242 → Rossendale 1292). By this etymology, the final element would refer to the deep valley of the R. Irwell and the Celtic elements to the surrounding moorland, but this etymology, proposed by Ekwall in *PNLa*, must remain very doubtful. It has been noted that ROSSENDALE is the only Celtic name, among the few for places above the 500-foot contour, which refers to a truly remote place; Ekwall himself later withdrew his earlier suggestion, although it has subsequently been revived. For the survival of a Celtic territorial name, compare *MAKERFIELD*. The name survives in THE FOREST OF ROSSENDALE, a major area of medieval forest (see introduction p. 20).

Rosthwaite horses' meadow (ON hross + ƿveit → Rostwhait 1609).

Roughlee Booth the rough *lēah* (OE rūh + lēah → Rughley 1296). The name suggests a clearing in the woodland of Pendle Chase and would be comparatively late (see introduction p. 21); it survives, with the addition of ON buð, 'hut, dairy farm', as the name of a township. The *OGDEN BROOK* or *PENDLE WATER* is here also known as the ROUGHLEE WATER.

Rowton Brook (R) roaring brook (ON rauta + -nde (present participle) + OE brōc → La Routandebrok

1323 → Rowtane 1537).

Royley *lēah* where rye is grown (OE rȳge + lēah → Rylegh 1325).

Royton *tūn* where rye is grown (OE rȳge + tūn → Ritton 1226 → Ryton 1260 → Ruyton 1327 → Royton 1577).

Rufford the rough ford (OE rūh + ford → Ruchford 1212 → Roughford 1328). The ford was evidently where the road from Mawdesley crossed the R. Douglas. RUFFORD was in the parish of Croston until it gained its own church in 1793. The Croston road crosses the river further north, and the name may therefore imply some distinction between the different crossing-points.

Rusholme (at) the rushes (OE risc, rysc + -um (dative pl.) → Russum 1235 → Ryssham 1316 → Rysholme 1551). This Manchester suburb is in low-lying land and its inflectional ending has been confused with ON *holmr*, 'water-meadow', which suits the nature of the site. The same element is found in other names in the Manchester area, notably in neighbouring *LEVENSHULME*, which would aid the confusion.

Rusland Hroald's or Hrolfr's land (ON Hróald(r)/Hrólf(r) + -es (possessive),+ land → Rolesland 1336 → Rwseland 1537).

S

Sabden the valley where fir-trees grow (OE sæppe + denu → Sapeden c.1140 → Sabdenbank 1504). The valley is that through which flows the SABDEN BROOK; the village stands on the brook.

St. Annes on Sea The place takes its name from the church, built in 1872-73, which is dedicated to St. Anne. The church was the first building to be constructed in a new planned town. The site was formerly called Kilgrimol c.1190, 'Kel-grim's hollow' (ON Kelgrim(r) + hol), but in 1532 a witness testified that Kilgrimol's churchyard was 'worne into the sea 2 or 3 miles'. The tidal patterns were changed by the dredging of the R. Ribble to allow large vessels to reach the port of Preston, and the coast became re-established. See *LYTHAM*.

St. Helens. The place takes its name from the chapel dedicated to St. Helen, first mentioned in 1552. The chapel of ease was probably of

129

medieval origin; it stood at the junction of the Warrington-Ormskirk and Prescot-Ashton roads. Four different buildings have occupied the site, of which the third, 1816-1916, was dedicated to St. Mary. Saxton makes the simple confusion of '-n-' with '-u-' in calling it Sct. Elyus chap. on his 1577 map.

St. Michael's on Wyre The place takes its name from the church dedicated to St. Michael, whose existence can be inferred from the DB name Michelscherche. As the modern name suggests, the village stands on the R. *WYRE* (Sancti Michaelis super Wirum c.1195 (Latin)).

Salesbury *burh* by SALE WHEEL (SALE + -s (possessive) + OE burh, in the form byrig (dative) → Salesbyry, Salebyry 1246). SALE WHEEL is the name of a pool in the R. Ribble; the name means 'pool where willows grow' (OE salh + wæl → Salewelle 1296). The village stands on a 475 foot hill which drops to the river two miles to the north where SALESBURY HALL stands. The second element here probably has the sense of 'town'; in early records the name is frequently found without '-s-'. The sense of '*burh* by the willows', which does not rely upon an existing name, has also been proposed.

Salford ford by willow-trees (OE salh + ford → Salford DB). The name refers to a crossing-point of the R. Irwell, on which the town stands. SALFORD is also the name of one of the county's six hundreds.

Salt Ayre See *AYRE*.

Saltcotes ? hut where salt is made. In her unpublished thesis, Miss Wise notes the forms Snartsalte 12th.c. → Swartsalte 14th.c. and compares ON svarta-salt, 'salt derived from sea-water', as opposed to ON hvita-salt. She postulates a development Swartsalt → Swartsaltcotes → Saltcotes, where OE cot, 'cottage, hut', has been added. The earliest form would then show '-n-' as an error for '-u-'. The hamlet stands in low ground by the R. Ribble. The salt-industry is thought to have died out about the middle of the eighteenth century here.

Salter ? salt shieling (OE salt + ON erg → Salter 1612). The name is recorded late, but it may suggest a building for the storage of salt. The name appears in the hamlets of LOWER, MIDDLE and HIGHER SALTER and in SALTER FELL, over which runs a track to Slaidburn, Yks.

Salwick *wīc* among the willow-trees (OE salh + wīc → Saleuuic DB → Salewic 1201 → Salwyk 1298). Now the name of a hall and of a station on the Preston-Blackpool railway line, SALWICK was a hamlet on Yates' 1786 map. It stands in low-lying land, now the course of the Lancaster Canal.

Samlesbury ? *burh* on a shelf of land (OE sceamol + -es (possessive) + burh, in the form byrig (dative) → Samerisberia 1179 (Latin) → Samelesbure 1188 → Samlesbiry 1246). The original settlement was probably around the church which stands by the R. Ribble, at the foot of the 168 foot ridge to which the first element may refer. The derivation from OE sceamol, however, involves taking as base later forms of the name in 'sh-', such as Shamplesbiry 1246, which, though not uncommon, are far less frequent than forms in 's-'. If the 's-' forms are original, the etymology is less certain. There is much variation in the representation of the first element in early records – e.g. Sambisbury c.1300, Sammysburi 1524, Samsbury 1577. There is today no village around the church; the main settlement moved to the south, to SAMLESBURY BOTTOMS, (OE botm, 'valley bottom', here referring to the valley of the R. Darwen in which the hamlet stands), where a community grew up around the cotton-mill which was built there c.1784.

Sankey Brook (R) ? holy river (Celt. *sancio → Sonchi c.1180 → Sanki 1202). The name is probably of Celtic origin, although the etymology is doubtful. The river (Sanki 1202) gave its name to GREAT SANKEY (Sonchi c.1180 → Sanki 1212→ Great Sonky 1325), LITTLE SANKEY and SANKEY BRIDGES.

Satterthwaite clearing by a mountain pasture (ON sǽtr + þveit → Saterthwayt 1336).

Savick Brook (R) etymology doubtful (Savoch 1190 → Savock c.1200). It has been suggested that the name contains Celt. *sab-, cognate with OE sæp, 'juice, sap', with the Celt. suffix '-āco-', used to form place- and river-names.

Sawrey the muddy places (ON saur(r) + -ar (pl.) → Sourer 1336 → Sawrayes c.1535). The hamlets of NEAR SAWREY (Narr Sawrey 1656) and FAR SAWREY (Far Sawrey 1657) are in a small valley which extends between Esthwaite Water and Lake Windermere; the name evidently refers to the low-lying nature of the land. The derivation from an inflected ON form attests the presence of a large Scandinavian element in the population (cf. *WINDERMERE*). The inflectional ending has later been confused with ON vrá, 'nook, corner of land'.

Scaitcliffe (Sclateclyff 1527 → Scaitclyff 1535). Both 'boundary hill' (ON skeið + klif) and 'slate hill' (ME slate, sclate + OE clif) have been suggested for this Accrington suburb.

Scaleber hut on a hill (OWScand. skáli + ON berg → Scaleberge 1202). The first element is indicative of Norwegian settlement.

Scales hut (OWScand. skáli). The name of two places:
(1) north-west of Aldingham (Scales 1269);
(2) *NEWTON*-WITH-SCALES (Skalys 1501). The word is indicative of Norwegian settlement. Compare *SCHOLES*.

Scarisbrick Skar's slope (ON Skar + -es (possessive) + OWScand. brekka → Scharisbrec c.1200 → Skaresbrek 1238 → Scarisbrick c.1240). The reference may be to the slight rise between two streams near which stands SCARISBRICK HALL. The personal name is often said to be Danish, but the second element is indicative of an area of Norwegian settlement.

Scarth Hill gap in the hill (ON skarð → Scarth c.1190 → Scarth Hill 16th.c.). The reference is not immediately clear. The hill is a 300-foot high point of the rising ground south-east of Ormskirk over which passes the Rainford-Ormskirk road.

Scholes hut (OWScand. skáli → Scholes 1332). The word is characteristic of Norwegian settlement – compare *SCALES*. The form here cited is for SCHOLES near Wigan but SCHOLES is a common minor name in the county.

Scorton *tūn* in or by a ravine (OE *scora/ON skor + OE tūn → Scourton 1550). The village is on the lower slopes of a hill which rises sharply to a height of 705 feet east of the R. Wyre. The OE word has the senses both of 'river-bank' and of 'precipitous slope', senses which suit the nature of the site better than ON skor, 'rift in a rock or precipice', but the formal development appears at least to have been influenced by the ON word.

Scotforth ford used by the Scots (OE Scot(t) + ford → Scozforde DB → Scotford 1212). The place was probably named because it was on the route taken by the cattle-drovers from Galloway; compare *GALGATE*, which lies to the south on the same road. Some distinction from *BIGFORTH* may also have been intended. The change from '-rd-' to '-rth' in the second element is frequent in NCy forms.

Seaforth This place near Litherland takes its name from SEAFORTH HOUSE, the Litherland home of Sir John Gladstone. Gladstone gave the house its name when he and his wife moved there in 1813 because his wife was a member of the MacKenzie clan whose head at that time was Lord Seaforth.

Seathwaite the clearing by the lake (ON sær +þveit → Seathwhot 1592). The modern village of SEATHWAITE is on the Tarn Beck near its confluence with the R. Duddon, on the site named on Yates' 1786 map as Seathwaite Chapel. The reference of the first element is to SEATHWAITE TARN, at the head of the Tarn Beck.

Sefton *tūn* where rushes grow (ON sef + OE tūn → Sextone DB → Seffton 1222). The name suggests the character of the land by the R. Alt where the church and mill stand: compare *MAGHULL* on the opposite bank. The hamlet of SEFTON TOWN is on slightly higher ground to the south-west.

Shakerley the robbers' *lēah* (OE scēacere + lēah → Shakerlee c.1210). The meaning 'woodland glade' might seem most appropriate for the second element here, but scēacere is also found with words such as *tūn* in English names.

Shard Bridge gap (OE sceard → Sharde 1713). This bridge across the R. Wyre at Hambleton seems to take its name from a field-name. Wainwright notes four examples of shard in Hambleton minor names. The name antedates the bridge, which was built in 1860, and referred to the site of a former ford or ferry. It is often assumed that the ford was previously called Aldwath, 'the old ford' (OE ald + ON vað).

Sharoe the boundary-ridge, or the ridge where the districts meet (OE scearu + hōh → Sharou, Shayrawe 1502).

Shaw wood (OE sceaga → Shaghe 1555). The element is also common in minor names.

Shevington *tūn* by a ridge (Welsh cefn + OE tūn → Shefinton c.1225 → Shevyngton 1312). The village is on a slope north of the R. Douglas, below SHEVINGTON MOOR. Possibly the ridge was called cefn by the Anglo-Saxons, who did not understand the meaning of the Celtic word; the name would then have the meaning 'tūn on the ridge called CEFN'. In *EPN* Ekwall notes that 'localities called Shevynlegh and Shevynhulldiche are mentioned 1329 and 1362 near SHEVINGTON'.

Shireshead the upper end of the shire (OE scīr + -es (possessive) + hēafod → Shireshead 1577). The place is near the northern boundary of Amounderness hundred.

Shooter (R) the stream used as a sewer (OE *scitere → Schiter 1334). The name is an agent-noun for OE scite, 'dung'.

Shore precipitous slope (OE *scor(a) → Shore 1324), referring to the hillside on which the hamlet stands.

Shuttleworth gated enclosure (OE scyt(t)els + worð → Suttelsworth 1227→ Shuttelesworthe 1296). The force of the first element is debatable – 'enclosure made of bars of a certain kind' has also been suggested as the meaning of the name. The forms given above are for the hamlet north of Ramsbottom, but the name survives also as a minor name in SHUTTLEWORTH HALL, near Hapton (Sutliswort, Scuteliworth 1300).

Silverdale the silver valley (OE seolfor + dæl → Selredale 1199 → Siuerdelege 1241 → Siluerdale c.1330). The place gains its name from the grey limestone of the crags around the village. The name appears also in nearby SILVERDALE GREEN.

Simm's Cross This Widnes suburb grew up at a meeting-point of roads where a cross stood. The first part of the name is probably through later association with a local family – compare *HUNT'S CROSS*.

Simonstone the stone building belonging to Sigemund (OE Sigemund + -es (possessive) + stān → Simondeston 1278). Alternatively, the sense may be 'Sigemund's stone', perhaps referring to some boundary-mark.

Simonswood Sigemund's wood (OE Sigemund + -es (possessive) + wudu → Simonddeswode 1190). The name refers to an area of woodland which was presumably held by a thegn before the Norman Conquest but which eventually became part of the demesne forest of south Lancashire.

Singleton ? *tūn* with shingles, i.e. wooden roofing tiles (ME *shingel + OE tūn → Singletun DB → Schingeltona 1169 (Latin)). By this etymology, the name would originally have begun with 'sh-', but this would

133

have been replaced by 's-', representing the Norman pronunciation of the name. An alternative etymology, involving a word recorded in use only from 1578, is ME *shingel, 'shingle, pebbles'. Forms in 's-' are frequent (e.g. Sengelton 1200, Sengleton 1330, Sinkiltun/Syngelton 1597) and may show influence, if not derivation, from OE *sengel, 'bundle, tuft' (the exact meaning is uncertain), which has been proposed as the etymology for the place in Sussex called Singleton.

Skelmersdale Skelmer's valley (Skelmer + -es (possessive) + ON dalr → Schelmeresdele DB). The reference may be to the valley of the R. Tawd – compare *DALTON*. The personal name is given here in a ME form, but it probably goes back to an ON *Skjaldmarr.

Skelwith the resounding ford (ON skjallr + vað → Schelwath 1246). SKELWITH FORCE is a waterfall on the R. Brathay, with ON fors, 'waterfall', as the final element.

Skerton *tūn* by the reef (ON sker + OE tūn → Schertune DB → Escartonam 1094 (Latin) → Scarton 1098 → Skerton 1200). The old village stands on the R. Lune opposite a low flat islet called Cow Shard.

Skippool the ship-pool i.e. anchorage or harbour (ON skip + OE pōl → Skippoles 1330). The place was formerly an important harbour. Ekwall argues that the place takes its name from the stream which enters the R. Wyre at this point and that pōl has therefore the sense of 'stream' here. In her unpublished thesis, however, Miss Wise notes that

this stream was called the Skipton or Skippon Brook in the 16th.c., a name which has survived to the present day; hence pōl refers to the pool where the two rivers meet, and Skipton is presumably from a minor settlement-name.

Slyne slope (OE *slinu → Sline DB), referring to the ridge on which the village stands. See *HEST*.

Smithills the smooth hill (OE smēðe + hyll → Smythell 1322).

Snape Green the poor pasture (ME snape → Snape c.1260). OE *snæp, 'boggy piece of land', would also suit the site.

Sollom the muddy enclosure (OE sol + ON *hegn → Solaynpul c.1200 → Solame 1372 → Solom 1554). The above etymology would suit the site, in low land west of the R. Douglas. ON sol, 'the sun', referring to a sunny site, usually a hill, has also been suggested.

Soutergate the shoemaker's road (ON sutari + gata → Soutergate 1332).

Southport Southport developed as a town only in very recent times. Yates' 1786 map marks *NORTH MEOLS* as the main settlement in this area (see also *CHURCHTOWN*). The district to the south, between Birkdale and Little London, was known as South Hawes. Here in 1792 William Sutton of North Meols built a hotel of driftwood. This was replaced by a stone building where, at a public dinner in 1798, the place was named 'South Port' by a Dr. Barton of Hoole. The site of the hotel was near the crossing of Lord Street and Duke Street today. The reason for the choice of name is not clear. 'South' may suggest a situation in relation to the 'north port' of Preston or continue the first element of South Hawes, in contradistinction to North Meols; the second element may suggest that 'Duke' Sutton envisaged a port to rival Preston or merely felt that it would be a better name for a fashionable watering-place than 'Hawes'.

Sowerby the marshy *bўr* (ON saurr + bўr → Sorbi DB → Sourby pre-1248). The form survives in the parish-name, *INSKIP*-WITH-SOWERBY, and in the minor name, SOWERBY HALL.

Speke brushwood (OE sp ēc → Spec DB → Speke 1252). The usual sense of sp ēc is 'small branch, twig, tendril'.

Spotland a small piece of land (OE *spot + land → Spotlond c.1180). There appears to be some connexion between the first element of this name and that of the SPODDEN BROOK (not named on the OS map) which flows through SPOTLAND (Spotbrok 13th.c. → Spodden 1577). The earliest form of the latter would suggest 'small piece of land by a brook' (OE br ōc), with later forms showing the addition of OE denu, 'valley'; but OE spūtan, 'to spout', has also been proposed.

Staining the place of the stone (OE st ān/ON steinn + -*ing* → Staininghe DB → Steyninges 1211 → Staining 1246). The above etymology suggests that the second element is the place-name forming suffix -*ing* and

that the first element is st ān, probably 'boundary-stone'. An alternative, perhaps supported by the plural form of 1211, is that the second element is the -*ingas* suffix and the first the personal name St ān, 'the people associated with St ān'; the name would then be evidence of early Anglo-Saxon settlement. The form of the first element shows influence from ON.

Stainton *tūn* where there are stones or boulders (OE st ān/ON steinn + OE tūn → Steintun DB → Staynton 1269). Ekwall comments that there were many stones found on the village green here. The first element shows ON influence on 'what was clearly originally an OE name.

Stalmine the fishing-pool by the mouth of the river (OE stell + ON mynni → Stalmine DB). The village is on a slight rise in flat country near the mouth of the R. Wyre. The second element suggests that stell has the sense of 'pool', and 'place for catching fish' is its usual meaning in place-names. But stell can also mean 'enclosure', and is here formally indistinguishable from OE stall, 'place'. Since the village is about two miles from the river, this sense cannot be ruled out. See *STAYNALL*.

Standen the stony valley (OE st ān + denu → Standen 1258), referring to the Pendleton Brook on which HIGHER and LOWER STANDEN and STANDEN HALL are situated. The brook is described as 'Aqua de Standene' in c.1200.

Standish the stony pasture (OE st ān + edisc → Stanesdis 1178 → Stanedisch 1253). The second element has the sense of 'enclosure, enclosed park'. Some confusion is indicated in the forms Stanedich 1213 (OE dīc, 'ditch') and Standigh 1327. The village is on high ground, dropping to the R. Douglas in the east. See *LANGTREE*.

Stanley Gate The hamlet takes its name from the Stanley family of Bickerstaffe.

Stanycliffe the stony hill (OE stānig + clif → Staniclive 13th.c.).

Staveley the wood where staves were obtained (OE stæf + lēah → Stavelay 1282).

Staynall the stony hollow/hollow where there is a boundary-stone (OE stān/ON steinn + OE/ON hol → Staynole 1190). The village is on a small hill on the east bank of the R. Wyre. See *STALMINE*.

Siddal Moor the wide nook of land (OE sīd + halh → Sydall 1548) to which has been added OE mōr, 'moor'.

Sidegarth wide enclosure (OE sīd + ON garðr → Sydeyarth 1322 → Sideyard 1458). The later form shows influence from OE geard, 'enclosure', an element more common in later field-names.

Stidd the place where the chapel is (OE stede → St. Saviour del Stude in Riblisdale pre-1246 → Stede 1276 → le Sted 1362). The word means generally 'place, site, locality' but the reference here seems clearly to the site of the hospital of St. Saviour acquired by the Knights Hospitallers; the hospital lost its endowments and ceased to function as a

charitable institution in the early fourteenth century, but the chapel remains. The modern name derives from a by-form, styde, which, in the earliest form cited, shows the rounded vowel '-u-', later to be unrounded to '-i-'.

Stodday the enclosure for horses (OE stōd + haga → Stodhae c.1200 → Stodaih c.1205 → Stodhaye c.1235). See *ASHTON*.

Stonyhurst the stony hill (OE stānig + hyrst → Stanyhurst 1358 → Stonyhirst 1577), now the name of a famous school in extensive grounds on high land near the junction of the rivers Hodder and Ribble.

Storrs Moss land growing with brushwood (ON storð → ?Estrodis 1210 → Stordis 1243 → the Storthes c.1350 → Storres c.1590). Some influence from OE strōd, 'marshy land overgrown with brushwood', is evident in the earliest forms and probably points to an OE origin. The reference is to mossland (OE mos, 'bog, swamp') east of Silverdale. The name or the same element is also seen in *YEALAND STORRS*, at the northern edge of STORRS MOSS.

Strangeways the area subject to strong flooding (OE strang + wæsc → Strangwas 1322 → Strangways 1326 → Strangeways 1546). The place is on a tongue of land between the rivers Irk and Irwell; wæsc has the sense of 'flooding, wash' but is also found in late ME in the sense of 'sandbank which the sea floods at high tide'. The name has been modified at a late date by folk-etymology.

Stretford the ford on the road (OE strǣt + ford → Stretford 1212). Strǣt usually refers to a Roman paved road, in this case the road from Deva (Chester) to Mamucium (Manchester); the ford marked the crossing point of the R. Mersey, at the site of the modern Crossford Bridge.

Stubbins a clearing (OE *stubbing → Stubbyns Halle 1559). The form is frequent in minor names.

Stub Hall tree-stump (OE stubb → Stub 1212). HALL is a late addition, Yates marking the hamlet as Stub in 1786.

Studlehurst the hill where horses are kept (OE stōd + hyll + hyrst → Stodelhirl 1246 → Stodilhirst c.1280). The name appears to have been originally 'horse-stud hill', OE stōd + hyll, to which was added OE hyrst, 'hillock, mound', at a later stage when the second element had become obscure. Both HIGHER and LOWER STUDLEHURST are on a slope to the south of the R. Ribble.

Subberthwaite the clearing belonging to, or near, a place called *SULBY (ON sól + berg + ꝥveit → Sulbythwayt 1284 → Soberthwayt 1538). The first part of the name is a lost place-name, but the meaning may have been 'sunny hill'. Alternatively, it may have originally been 'Suli's býr', ON Suli + býr, and have been influenced later by berg.

Sudden the south valley (OE súð + denu → Sothden 13th.c. → Sudden 13th.c.). The place is on the SUDDEN BROOK, near its confluence with the R. Roch. Its identification as 'south' may be relative to the R. Roch, in distinction to *NORDEN*, four miles north-west, on the opposite side of the river.

Summerseat the shieling used in the summer (ON sumarr + sætr → Sumersett 1556).

Sunbrick the slope where pigs are kept (ON svin + brekka → Swinebroc 1269 → Swynbreke 1282 → Sonbrek 1418). The early forms suggest a rationalisation by English speakers under OE swīn + brōc, 'the swine-brook'. The first element in particular has undergone further change.

Sunderland outlying or detached land (OE sundorland → Sinderlaund/ Sunderlond 1246). The forms quoted are for the hamlet situated on the northern bank of the R. Lune near its mouth, on a small peninsula of land whose southern tip is SUNDERLAND POINT. The form is seen also in the minor name, SUNDERLAND HALL, on the south bank of the R. Ribble, (Sunderland 1172).

Sutton tūn in the south (OE súð + tūn → Sutton 1200). The township lies to the south of St. Helens. The form occurs in other names nearby, including SUTTON MANOR and SUTTON LEACH (OE *læc, 'stream'), the latter apparently Yates' Toad Leach (? The old LEACH) of 1786. The name SUTTON is, however, quite frequently found in the county.

Swarthmoor the black moor (OE sweart + mōr → Swartemore 1537

137

→ Swarthmore 1537). The hamlet takes its name from a large tract of moorland to the south, marked on Yates' 1786 map but now drained.

Swinton *tūn* where pigs are kept (OE swīn + tūn → Suinton 1258). See *PENDLEBURY.*

T

Tame (R) etymology doubtful (Brit. *tamo- → Tome 1292 → Tame 1322). It has been suggested that the word may be related to OIr. temen, 'dark', and mean 'the dark river'.

Tarbock brook where hawthorntrees grow (OE þorn + brōc → Torboc DB). The place is by the Ditton Brook. The name has undergone considerable modification, but the above etymology is confirmed by forms such as Thorboc 1242, Thornebrooke c.1244. 'Th-' has become 'T'- under French influence, there being no French equivalent to OE 'th'; 'n' has been lost in the 'nb' combination and the second 'r' has been lost through dissimilation, in distinction to the preceding 'r'. The change from 'Tor-' to 'Tar-' was evidently under way when the name was recorded as Terbok 1386, preparing for the later change of 'er' to 'ar' (compare person/parson). Compare *TARNBROOK.*

Tarleton Tharaldr's *tūn* (ON Þaraldr + OE tūn → Tarleton c.1200).

Tarnacre field where cranes are found (ON trani + akr → Tranaker c.1210). The name is seen only in the parish-name of UPPER *RAW-CLIFFE*-WITH-TARNACRE and in the minor name TARNACRE HALL.

Tarnbrook ? brook where hawthorn trees grow (OE þorn + brōc → Tyrnbrok 1323). The form is late and the etymology must be doubtful, although the name was clearly originally a stream-name, probably referring to the TARNBROOK WYRE on which the hamlet stands. On the formal development of the first element, compare TARBOCK. Ekwall notes the desirability of derivation from ON tjǫrn, 'tarn, small lake', but there is no such lake in the area. The first element recurs in TARNSYKE CLOUGH, with OE sīc, 'small stream', and OE *clōh, 'deep valley'.

Tarn Hows hills where the lake is situated (ON tjǫrn + haugr → Ternehowys 1538).

Tatham *hām* of Tāta (OE Tāta + ham → Tathaim DB → Tatham c.1197). The DB form may show influence from ON heim, 'home, homestead, estate'.

Taunton *tūn* on a spit of land (OE tang, tong + tūn → Tongton 1246 → Tounton 1276 → Taunton 1422). It has been plausibly suggested that the reference is to the tongue of land formed by the TAUNTON BROOK and the R. Medlock, which meet near the place. On the first element, compare the minor name, *TONGE HALL*, Middleton.

Tawd (R) etymology doubtful (Tavelede c.1240 → Tauelet/Tauelde 1400 → Taude 1577). Lacking early forms, Ekwall proposed that the name was a back-formation from the OE phrase æt þon aldan ford, 'at the old ford, an OE place-name which could have developed to 'at owd ford' and hence to 'Tawd ford, 'at the old ford', an OE place-Lenney, rightly criticising this etymology, preferred to leave the etymology doubtful but suggested a possible connexion with the root tevá, teu, 'to swell', which has been proposed for the rivers Taw and Tay. Welsh taw, 'silent', has also been suggested for the former. It might seem plausible to propose a Celtic etymology for the river, in view of the preponderance of Celtic river-names in the county. The development may, however, have been influenced also by OE tæfl/tefle for which a range of meanings has been proposed, including 'plateau', 'the flat stones forming the track of a ford' and 'land in dispute', the latter deriving from the general sense of 'to argue, strive' which might itself

be appropriate. Early forms may also show identification of the final syllable with OE hēafod, 'head'. See *TAWDBRIDGE*.

Tawdbridge Originally, the ford over the R. *TAWD* (TAWD + OE ford → Taueldeford 1246 → Taldeford mid-13th.c.). *VCH* says that this was later called Tawdbridge, though no reason for this statement is given. Two places called TAWDBRIDGE are marked on the 1848 OS map, the modern name near Lathom and one near Hoscar.

Templand etymology doubtful (Templand 1491).

Tewitfield the marsh where the lapwing is found (OE tew(h)it + ON mýrr → Tikwitmyre 1346 → Tewhitmyre c.1388 → Tuwhitefeld 1519). The second element has later been replaced by OE feld, 'open country'. It has also been suggested, less plausibly, that the etymology may have been ON hvitr + mýrr, 'the bright marsh', the initial 'T'-deriving from the definite article and perhaps influenced by the preposition æt introducing the place-name phrase.

Thatto Heath the torrential stream (OE pēote + wella → Thetwall 12th.c. → Thattow Heath 1786). The full range of meaning of the first element includes 'fountain, water-pipe and conduit'. OE hæð, 'heath', has been added at a later stage.

Thingwall the field where the assembly meets (ON þing + vǫllr → Tingwella 1177 → Thingwalle 1212). The name has the same origin and sense as Manx Tynwald. It points to a distinctively Norse system of administration in the area, referring to the assembly of the wapentake. The name does not appear on the OS map – it survived in THING-WALL HALL, whose hill-site might have been the original assembly-hill. The hall is in Knotty Ash, close to West Derby, the centre of West Derby Hundred. The second element has been confused with OE wella, 'well, spring', a confusion perhaps aided by the example of nearby *CHILDWALL*. The earliest form shows OF 'T-' for OE 'Th-'.

Thistleton *tūn* where the thistles grow (OE ʓistel + tūn → Thistilton 1212).

Thornham *hām* by the hawthorn tree (OE ʓorn + hām → Thornham 1246).

Thornley the clearing by or among thorn-trees/the clearing overgrown with thorns (OE ʓorn + lēah → Thorenteleg 1202 → Thornedlay pre-1278 → Thornley 1327). The village is on the north-west slope of Longridge Fell and the clearing was therefore in the Bowland chase. The early forms suggest that the first element was an adjectival derivative such as *ʓornede. See *WHEATLEY*.

Thornton *tūn*, or enclosure, of thorns (OE ʓorn + tūn), the name of two places:
(1) near Sefton (Torentun DB → Thorinton 1212); the DB form shows OF 'T-' for OE 'Th-' – spellings in 'T-' are frequent;
(2) near Poulton (Torentun DB → Thorneton 1246). On initial 'T-'

for 'Th-', see (1) above. The village is often grouped with the coastal settlement of CLEV-ELEYS, the whole being called THORNTON CLEVELEYS. No etymology has been suggested for CLEVELEYS, which is marked on Yates' 1786 map as Clevelas House. If it is not a personal name, it might be OE clif + læs, 'meadow-land by a slope'. *VCH,* however, states that the name replaced the older Ritherham/Ritherholme (OE hriðer + ON hamm, 'ox-meadow').

Threaphaw Fell hill over which there was a dispute (OE prēap + ON haugr → Trepehowe, Threphaw, Threpshowe c.1350). The fell is on the boundary between Lancashire and Yorkshire.

Thrushgill the giant's ravine (ON ʓurs + OWScand. gil → Thursclogh c.1350 → Thursgyll c.1350). The ravine is evidently the gorge through which the R. Hindburn flows. The change in the position of '-r-' has led to or resulted from association of the first element with OE ʓrysce, 'thrush', but the word refers to some supernatural being such as a giant or demon, perhaps with some pagan overtones. The earliest form here cited has OE clōh, 'ravine', as second element and could indicate that the name is OE rather than ON in origin, with OE ʓyrs, 'giant', as the original first element.

Thurland Castle ? Thor's land (ON ʓor + -es (possessive) + land → Thurland 1465). The name is recorded late and refers to the castle crenellated in 1402 by Sir Thomas

Tunstall.

near Middleton.

Thurnham (at) the thorn-bushes (OE þyrne, in the form þyrnum (dative pl.) → Teirnun DB → Thurnum 1160). The 'T-' for 'Th-' in the DB form represents French pronunciation. The inflectional ending has later been confused with OE *hām*.

Thwaite Flat village on a level piece of ground (ON þveit + flat → Wateflatt c.1535).

Tilberthwaite the clearing belonging to a place called *TILLESBURGH (OE Tilhere + -s (possessive) + burh + ON þveit → Tildesburgthwait 1196 → Tilburthwait 1412). The first part of the name is evidently a lost place-name, 'Tilli's *burh';* the personal name is perhaps a shortened form of a compound name such as Tilhere.

Tockholes etymology doubtful (Cokolles 1199 → Tocholis c.1200 → Thocol 1246). The second element is OE hol, 'hollow, depression', referring to its position on the western slope of a hill. It has been suggested that the first element is a personal name, OE Tocca or ON Tóki. The earliest form is evidently a result of scribal confusion of 'C-' and 'T-'.

Tonge tongue of land (OE tang, tong → Tange 1212 → Tonge 1226). TONGE FOLD and TONGE MOOR, the 'sheepfold' and 'moor' belonging to TONGE preserve on the modern OS map the name of the hamlet north of BOLTON marked on Yates' 1786 map on land between the Tonge and Bradshaw brooks. TONGE HALL is a minor name

Torrisholme *holmr* belonging to Thorald (ON þóraldr/þorold+ holmr → Toredholme DB → Turoldesholm 1204 → Thoraldesholm 1206 → Thorisholm 1310 → Torisholm 1322). The place is situated at the south end of a ridge, above low-lying country. A number of early forms show '-ham', in confusion with OE hām or hamm, instead of '-holm'.

Torver the turf-roofed hut (ON torf + erg → Thoruergh c.1195 → Torvergh 1246 → Torver 1537). Although the first element is usually used in ON with reference to turf-roofed buildings, the possibility that the name means 'peat shieling' has also been suggested.

Tottington *tūn* associated with Totta (OE Totta + -ing + tūn → Totinton 1212 → Totington 1233). The name is generally accepted as a possible -ingatūn name and hence as evidence of early settlement (See introduction p. 46). The first element is one of the commonest OE personal names, evidenced from an early date, and the village is situated near a Roman road. However, it has been pointed out that the village is on a hill and that OE *tōt, 'a look-out, look-out hill', frequently formally indistinguishable from Totta, is a possible first element.

Tottleworth Tottla's enclosure (OE *Tottla + worð → Tottleworth c.1204). The hamlet lies between hills and OE *tōt-hyll, 'look-out hill', has been proposed as first element; the name would then mean 'enclosure by a look-out hill.'

141

However, OE worð occurs most frequently with personal names.

Towneley the clearing belonging to the town (OE tūn + lēah → Tunleia c.1200 → Touneley 1290), the name of a hall and its park, both open to the public, near Burnley. This region, with its settlement, probably joined the township of Burnley in the 13th.-14th.cs. Compare *TUNLEY.*

Town Green the green belonging tc the township – in this case to the township fo Aughton (Town Green 1786). The name is frequently found in early records (e.g. Toungrene mid-13th.c.), but was clearly a frequent minor name which identified the greens of different towns – in the case of the mid-13th.c. example cited, HARLETON.

Toxteth Park Toki's landing-place (ON Tóki + stoð → Stochestede DB → Tokestath 1212). The name does not appear on the OS map, but is notable as a minor name for a district brought under forest-law in c.1088-1102. The personal name is Danish; the landing-place may have been on the R. Mersey or on the Dingle Brook.

Trafford the road-ford (OE stræt + ford → Stratford 1206 → Straforde 1212 → Trafford c.1200). The name is a variant of *STRETFORD* which lies to the south. The Norman form of the name was applied to the manor of TRAFFORD which was formed out of part of STRETFORD township. The name survives as OLD TRAFFORD, marked on Yates' 1786 map, and in TRAFFORD PARK. The latter appears in early records as Whittleswick

(Quitliswic 1251 → Whikelswike 1322), perhaps 'Cwichelm's farm' (OE Cwichelm + -es (possessive) + wīc). This area was acquired by the Trafford family in the 17th.c. and is now a large industrial estate whose main offices were formerly in TRAFFORD HALL.

Trawden the trough-shaped valley (OE trōg + denu → Trochdene 1296 → Troudene 1322). The reference appears to be to the river-valley in which the village stands. The name FOREST OF TRAWDEN recalls the area formerly under forest-law.

Treales ? the township of the court (Welsh tref + Brit. *lisso- → Treueles DB → Treules 1324 → Treeles 1431). The first element has the sense of 'farmstead, homestead, hamlet', the second of 'hall' and perhaps 'court, chief house of a district'. The relationship between the elements and their exact sense may be debated, but the name is significant as being almost the only certain example of a Celtic place-name in the county which evidences building rather than physical features. It therefore suggests an unusually tenacious Celtic presence in the area. Wainwright has also drawn attention to the field-name, Chester Field, which, while not necessarily evidence of the site of the hall, does suggest a spot for archaeological investigation. See *ROSEACRE, WHARLES.*

Trough of Bowland See *BOWLAND.*

Trunnah ? the circular enclosure (OE *trun + haga → Truno 1271 → Trunnall 1593). More early forms are needed to ascertain the second element.

Tunley the clearing belonging to the town (OE tūn + lēah → Tunleg 1246 → Tunlegh 1332). Compare *TOWN-ELEY*.

Tunstall the site of a farm (OE *tūn-stall → Tunestalle DB).

Turton Thor's *tūn* (ON Þor/Þur + OE tūn → Turton 1212).

Twiss Green the fork in a river (OE (ge)twis → Twisse 1258). GREEN

has been added later (Twistgrene 1565).

Twiston *tūn* at the fork of a river (OE twisla + tūn → Tuisleton 1102 → Tuystòn 1270). The village is in the middle of a tongue of land between the Ings Beck and a tributary stream.

Tyldesley Tilwald's *lēah* (OE Tilwald + -es (possessive) + lēah → Tildesleia c.1210). See *SHAKER-LEY*.

U

Ulnes Walton the *WALTON* belonging to Ulf (ON Ulf(r) + -es (possessive) + WALTON → Waleton 1203 → Ulneswalton 1285). The modern form is a spelling form. The local pronunciation of 'Oves' or 'Oos' Walton more faithfully reflects the original. The parish takes its name from Ulf de Walton, who lived c.1160. The possessive form was spelt Ulues, and the second '-u-' was confused with '-n-', a common confusion in early spelling. On the second part of the name, see *WALTON* where the various other WALTON's from which this had to be distinguished are listed.

Ulverston Wulfhere's/Ulfarr's *tūn*

(OE Wulfhere/ON Ulfarr + -es (possessive) + tūn → Vlureston DB → Oluestonam 1127 (Latin) → Ulverston c.1182). It is held locally that the place takes its name from an Anglo-Saxon nobleman who conquered Furness, but the identity of the owner of the *tūn* is unknown. It has also been suggested, again without evidence, that ULVERS-TON is the later name of the vill of Hougun, the name of the manor in DB in which most of Furness lay, which has been lost.

Unsworth Hund's enclosure (OE Hund + -es (possessive) + worð → Hundeswrth 1291 → Undesworth 1322).

143

Upholland land on a spur (OE hōh + land → Hoiland DB → Upholland 1226). The village is on a hillside; the land falls to Holland Moss in the south-west and the R. Douglas in the north-east. The site and name are distinguished from *DALTON*, three miles north-west. To HOLLAND, which continued to be used as the name long after 1226, was added the prefix, OE upp, 'higher'. See *DOWN-HOLLAND*.

Uplitherland See *LITHERLAND*.

Upper – For places which have UPPER as their first element, see the entry under the second part of the name.

Upton the higher *tūn* (OE upp + tūn → Upton 1251). The hamlet stands on higher land. It has been suggested that the name is of the 'upp-in-tune' type and means 'land higher up in the village'. It seems probable, however, that the first element is in distinction to nearby *CRONTON*, *APPLETON*, and particularly *DITTON* to the south-west on low-lying ground.

Urmston Urm's *tūn* (ODan. Urm + -es (possessive) + OE tūn → Wermeston 1194 → Urmeston 1212). The personal name is a distinctively ODan. form of OWScand. Ormr, seen in *ORMSKIRK*, and accords with other Danish forms in the names of the Manchester area.

Urswick village by the bison-lake (OE ūr + sǣ + wīc → Ursewica c.1150 (Latin)). The parish contains GREAT URSWICK (Magna Urswic 1180, Great Urswyk 1277) and LITTLE URSWICK (Parva Urswik 1257, Little Ursewyk 1299). Both are in a valley, and the former is by URSWICK TARN, perhaps the feature to which the name refers.

Vickerstown Following their purchase of the Barrow shipyard in 1896, Vickers Sons and Co. built a model town on Walney Island for their workmen and named the town after the company.

Vulcan Village The village is named after the Vulcan Works, founded by Robert Stephenson and Charles Tayleur in 1830, whose workers it was built to house.

W

Waddicar field where the woad-plant grows (OE wād + æcer → Wadacre 1246).

Walkden Wealaca's valley (OE Wealaca + denu → Walkeden 1325).

Walmer Bridge marshy ground where woodland grows (OE wald + ON mȳrr → Waldemurebruge 1251). BRIDGE is a later addition.

Walmersley *lēah* belonging to *WAL-MER; the first element would be an existing place-name made up of either OE wald + mere, 'lake by a wood' or OE wald + gemǣre, 'boundary of a wood' (WALMER + -es + lēah → Walmeresley 1262).

Walney Island island of quicksands (OE *wagen + ēg → Wagneiam 1127 (Latin) → Wannegia 1246 → Waghenay 1336 → Wawenay 1404 → Walney 1577). The name presents difficulties, but the above explanation seems preferable to the alternative, ON vǫgn + ey, 'grampus island'. The first element has been changed at a late stage of development on analogy to names in *Wal-* deriving from OE walh, 'serf'.

Walsden serf's valley (OE wal + -es (possessive) + denu → Walseden 1235).

Walthwaite clearing by a meadow (ON vǫllr + þ veit → Walthwayt c.1270).

Walton serf's *tūn* (OE walh + tūn). A common name, seen in
(1) WALTON-LE-DALE (Waletune DB → Walton in la Dale 1304); the dale here is Ribblesdale, since the town stands on a steep wooded bank above the R. Ribble, and the place is called Waletona in Ribbellesdale pre-1210 (on LE, see introduction, p. 43).
(2) WALTON-ON-THE-HILL (Waletone DB → Walton 1305), on a hill above the surrounding area with its parish church a familiar landmark (see *KIRKDALE*);
(3) *ULNES* WALTON (Waleton 1203 → Ulneswalton 1285);
(4) WALTON BRECK (in territorio de Walton' scilicet ad quemdam locum qui vocatur le Breche 1266), where a second word, OE brēc, 'land broken up for cultivation', or ON brekka, 'slope', has been added.
The word occurs in other names

145

which are today minor (e.g. WALTON HALL – Walletun DB) or lost (e.g. Walton Lees 13th.c.), hence the need for additional distinguishing terms.

Warbreck hill with cairn on top, i.e. a look-out hill (ON varða + brekka → Wardebrec c.1140 → Warthebrek 1324). The forms here given refer to Warbreck near Bispham, Amounderness, which is on a 100-foot ridge. The name also occurs near Liverpool.

Warcockhill etymology doubtful (Werkochull c.1250 → Warcockhill 1658). The second element is clearly OE hyll, 'hill'. It has been suggested that the first element is ME wer-cok, 'pheasant', although this is first recorded only in 1420. OE cocc, 'heap, hillock', is common with hill-names and difficult to distinguish from OE cocc, 'cock, woodcock', and, on this late evidence, the possibility of some compound of OE weard, 'watch'/ON varða, 'cairn, lookout' with OE cocc, or even OE cop, 'hill-top', cannot be totally discounted.

Wardle lookout hill (OE weard + hyll → Wardhul c.1193 → Wardhil 1198), an original hill name probably referring to the 1300-foot-high Brown Wardle Hill to the north-west of the village.

Wardleys (Warleys 1825), a small creek on the R. Wyre, but the former harbour of Poulton. If the name is old, it may be OE waroð + læs, 'pasture-land by the shore'.

Warrington tūn by a river-dam (OE wer + -ing + tūn → Walintune DB →

Werineton 1228 → Werington 1246 → Warryngton 1332). The Roman roads from Chester and London met here to cross the R. Mersey by a shallow ford. The settlement may be of British origin but there is no evidence to support the local antiquarian belief that the name is a corruption of Latin Veratinum and the evidence for an early settlement, taking the name as an -ingatūn name-form. is not strong.

Warton look-out tūn (OE weard + tūn). The name of two villages:
(1) in Lonsdale (Wartun DB), on the lower slopes of Warton Crag, a 534 foot hill with the remains of an ancient hill-fort, to which the first element may refer;
(2) near Lytham (Wartun DB) where there was a guide for the sands-crossing from Warton to Hesketh Bank. While this may explain the sense of the first element, the location makes derivation from OE waroð, warð, 'shore', equally possible.

Waterhouses Named after the 'Waterhouse', the former name of Medlock Hall, so called from its location by the R. Medlock. It is also known as DAISY NOOK, since it was chosen by the Oldham artist, Charles Potter, as the subject to illustrate Ben Brierley's poem, 'A Day Out, or A Summer Ramble to Daisy Nook'.

Waterloo This Liverpool suburb takes its name from the Royal Waterloo Hotel, which was founded in 1815 and named after the battle. The link with the hotel was lost when the hotel-name was shortened to the Royal Hotel.

Wavertree swaying tree (OE wæfre + trēow→ Wauretreu DB → Wavertre 1196). The possibility that the reference is to an aspen tree has been suggested and the fact that aspens still flourish in the area noted. However, dial. waver has the sense of 'an isolated young tree' (cf. *AINTREE, KNOTTY ASH*).

Weaste common (OF wast(e)).

Weeton *tūn* among willow-trees (OE wiðig + tūn → Widetun DB → Wytheton 1243 → Wyhton 1297 → Wytton 1329 → Weton 1341). See *PREESE.*

Wenning (R) the dark river (OE wann + *-ing* → Wenninga c.1175 Latin). See *WENNINGTON.*

Wennington *tūn* on the R. *WENNING* (WENNING + OE tūn → Wennigetun DB→Wenington 1212). The name presents some difficulties since there are two villages of this name. WENNINGTON is on the R. Wenning, but OLD WENNINGTON (Old Wenigton 1227), presumably the original township, is to the north-east, on the R. Greeta. No certain solution for this problem can be found, although it has been suggested that the village name may be independent of the river name — perhaps an *-ingatūn* type with OE Wenna — and the river-name perhaps even a back-formation. It would, however, be simpler to assume that Old Wennington was an older settlement renamed in terms of Wennington at a time when the derivation of the name from the river had been forgotten.

Werneth place where alders grow (Brit. *verno-* + -eto- → Wornyth c.1200 → Vernet c.1224 → Wyrnith 1323).

Wesham (at) the western houses (OE west + hūs + -um (dative pl.) → West(h)usum 1189 → Westsum 1327 → Wessum 1431). The place lies north-west of Kirkham and was probably an offshoot of that town; hence it is named in relation to Kirkham. See *MEDLAR'*

Westby the western *bȳr* (ON vestr + bȳr → Westbi DB). The hamlet lies to the west of Wrea Green. See *PLUMPTON.*

West Close Booth western enclosure (OE west + OF, ME clos → Westecloos 1324), to which ON bōth, 'hut, dairy farm', has been added; the earliest form is the name of a vaccary. There is today no village called WEST CLOSE and the name survives in the parish-name, *HIGHAM - WITH - WEST - CLOSE-BOOTH.*

West Derby the DERBY in the west (OE west + DERBY → Derbei DB); DERBY means '*bȳr* where deer are found' (ON *djúr* + bȳr). The place gave its name to one of Lancashire's six hundreds; the hundred was formerly called Derbyshire (Derbissyre 13th.c.). It is possible that WEST was added to distinguish the place from Derby, the county town of Derbyshire (Westderbi 1177).

West Didsbury See *DIDSBURY.*

Westhead the western hill (OE west + hēafod → Westheft c.1190 → Westheved c.1200). The name refers to the western part of the headland at the end of the ridge leading up to Scarth Hill.

Westhoughton *tūn* in a *halh* (OE halh + tūn → Halcton c.1210). WEST was added to the name (Westhalcton c.1240 → Westhalghton 1500) presumably to distinguish it from LITTLE HOUGHTON, near Eccles, a lost name. See also *HOUGHTON* and compare *HULTON* nearby, to the east.

Westleigh the western *lēah* (OE west + lēah → Westlegh 1238 → Westlay in Legh 1292). The place is north-west of *LEIGH*, from which it is distinguished. Compare *ASTLEY*.

Whalley *lēah* by a hill (OE *hwæl + lēah → Hwællleage 798 → Wallei DB). The village is in a gap between Clerk Hill the southern spur of Pendle Hill, and Whalley Nab (WHALLEY + ON nabbi, 'hill' → Nab 1579). The Nab is the eastern point of *BILLINGTON* HILL and was also called Belsetenab 13th.c.

Wharles (stone) circles (OE hwerfel + -as (pl.) → Quarlous 1249 → Werlows 1286). The name may refer to the same feature indicated by *ROSEACRE*, about a mile away to the north-west. Wainwright has drawn attention to five instances of the field-name Wheel Meadow in the neighbouring township of Newton-with-Scales. The 1286 form shows the substitution of OE hlāw + -as (pl.), 'mounds', for the inflectional ending, perhaps influenced by the higher ground to the east, west and north of the hamlet, and giving the sense 'mounds in a circle'. See *TREALES*.

Wheatley *lēah* where wheat is grown (OE hwǣte + lēah). The name of three villages:
(1) near Chipping (Watelei DB);
(2) near *BARLEY* (Weteley 1420), with which it is linked in the parish-name, BARLEY-WITH-WHEATLEY-BOOTH (Whitley in Haboothe 1502) and from which it is distinguished;
(3) WHEATLEY CARR (Wheteley carre 1464), where ON kjarr, 'marsh', forms the final element.

Whelley ? *lēah* where there is a stone-circle (OE hwēol + lēah → Quelley 1383 → Whelley 1553).

Wheelton *tūn* on a circular hill (OE hwēol + tūn → Weltonam c.1160 (Latin) → Wheleton c.1240 → Welton 1276).

Whinfield gorse-covered hill (ON *hvin + fjall → Quinfel' 1329 → Whinfell 1587). The first element is common in minor names – e.g. Whin Lane End, Whinney Hill and Whinney Heys, the site of Blackpool airport.

Whinfold Fell gorse-covered fell (ON *hvin + fjall → Whynfell c.1350). The modern second element is not recorded in early forms and could well be a remodelling of the original second element, ON fjall, on the basis of OE fald, 'fold, enclosure for animals'; if so, FELL was added once more at a later stage. Compare *WHINFIELD*.

Whiston the white stone (OE hwīt + stān → Quistan 1190 → Wytstan 1252 → Whistan 1272), referring to a local feature noted in early records.

Whitefield ? dry open pasture (OE hwīt + feld → Whitefeld 1292). The etymology is generally agreed, but the exact sense of OE hwīt, 'white', here may be debated.

Whiteray the bright nook (ON hvitr + vrá → Wytewra 1235 → Whitraye 1622). The name is found in a remote part of the fell-district, near the source of the R. Hindburn; it is a beck-and fell-name.

Whittingham hām of Hwita's people (OE Hwīt(a) + -ingahām → Witingheham DB → Whitingham 1200). The name is of the -ingahām type and is indicative of early Anglo-Saxon settlement (see introduction pp. 00).

Whittington the white tūn (OE hwīt + tūn → Witetune DB → Witington 1212). The name has been said to be an -ingatūn name, perhaps indicative of early Anglo-Saxon settlement, but the earliest form does not support that suggestion. The '-ng-' development is best explained as the development of a particular adjectival inflection, seen in the phrase æt þǣm hwītan tūne, 'at the white tūn', in which the combination '-nt-' has developed an intrusive '-g-'. However, the town was clearly important at the time of the Norman Conquest, being the centre of the lordship of Earl Tostig before 1066.

Whittle the white or bright hill (OE hwīt + hyll). The name of two places:
(1) WHITTLE-LE-WOODS (Witul c.1160 → Whithill in bosco 1327 → Whitle in the Wood 1381 → Whitle in le Woods 1565);
(2) WHITTLE HILL (Quitul 1292

→ Whittle 1612), a hill of 1,534 feet — with the loss of the distinctive form of the second element, HILL has again been added.

Whitworth the white enclosure (OE hwīt + worð → Whiteword 13th.c. → Whiteworth 13th.c.).

Widnes the wide promontory (OE wīd + ness → Wydnes c.1200). The headland is a promontory jutting out into the R. Mersey at a narrow point known as the Runcorn Gap. The size of the promontory has been reduced by blasting operations for the construction of the Widnes-Runcorn bridges.

Wigan etymology doubtful (Wigan 1199). The name may well be a shortened form of a Celtic name, such as tref Wigan, 'Wigan's home-stead', but a name of similar form in Huntingdonshire has been derived from OE wīc + -um (dative pl.), '(at) the dwellings'. If the Celtic etymology is accepted, the name would be a late Celtic compound, perhaps subsequently corrupted by the Anglo-Saxon settlers — compare *KENYON*. The town is on a Roman road and was called Coccium by the Romans. It was evidently a place of some importance from an early time, and there are names of Celtic origin nearby (see introduction p. 35). Antiquarians, attempting to associate King Arthur with south Lancashire, have sometimes proposed a derivation from OE wīg, 'war', or wiga, 'warrior', suggesting WIGAN as the site of one of Arthur's battles on a river called Douglas,· but this proposal has no justification; see *MARTIN MERE*.

Wilpshire ? the estate of someone nicknamed Wlips, 'the one who lisps' (OE wlips + scīr → Wlypschyre 1246 → Wylppeschyre 1300 → Wilpschire 1311). The first element is very doubtful; forms such as Lplipeshir, Lplipeshirebroc ('Wilpshire Brook') of. 1300 illustrate the difficulties of reconstructing the original form of the name. The sense of scīr is also debatable; it perhaps suggests a district with some degree of administrative independence.

Winder The name of two places:
(1) hamlet near Caton, 'the windy outcrop' (OE wind + hōh → Quinehou 1220 → Wyndergh 1301). The hamlet stands on a hill-slope. The second element has later been replaced by ON erg, 'hill-pasture', equally appropriate to the site;
(2) RAVEN WINDER, a hamlet in WINDER MOOR, a salt marsh by the shore of Morecambe Bay, 'the windy dairy-settlement' (ON vindr + erg → Winderghe e.13th.c. → Ravynse Wyndor 1491). RAVEN, a later addition, is probably the ON personal name Hrafn; the place is also called Chanon Wynder in 1491. The salt-marsh site prevents the application of the usual sense of erg, 'hill-pasture', but the marsh may not have provided any pasture – the sense may well be 'hut for shelter against the wind'.

Windermere Vinnunder's lake (OSwed. Vinnunder, in the form Vinandar (possessive) + OE mere → Winendemere c.1160 → Winandermer 1196). The edge of the lake forms the county boundary. The

retention of the ON possessive inflection in the name suggests a large Scandinavian element in the population of the area.

Windle windy hill (OE wind + hyll → Windhull 1201). This parish-name is seen also in the minor name WINDLESHAW, 'copse belonging to WINDLE' (WINDLE + OE sceaga → Windell Shaae Park 1548).

Winewall ? Wina's stream (OE Wina + wella → Wynewelle 1296 → Wynewall 1507). The name may refer to the Trawden Water on which the place stands, and TRAWDEN may be a later name. The etymology here proposed would suggest a first element pronounced 'win' rather than 'wine' and, if the suggestion that modern pronunciation is influenced by spelling is accepted, Celt. *winn, 'white, fair, holy', would be equally possible and appropriate.

Winmarleigh Winemær's lēah (OE Winemær + -es (possessive) + lēah → Wynemerislega 1212 (Latin) → Winmerleie c.1220).

Winstanley Wynstan's lēah (OE Wynstān + -es (possessive) + lēah → Vnstanesle 1206 → Winstanesle 1212 → Winstanlee c.1200).

Winster (R) (the river on) the left (ON vinstri → Winster c.1180). The river forms the boundary between Lancashire and Westmorland. The name implies a comparison – either with the R. Leven, which forms the western boundary of Cartmel, or with the R. Gilpin, We, which joins the R. Kent to the east of the R. WINSTER.

Winter Hill the hill which is used in winter (OE winter + hyll), referring to a hill of 1,498 feet.

Winton *tūn* among willow-trees (OE *wiðign + tūn → Wythynton 1284 → Wynton 1535). The site is low-lying and marshy. Compare *WITHINGTON*.

Winwick Wineca's *wīc* (OE Wineca + wīc → Winequic 1170 → Winewich 1204).

Wiswell marshy stream (OE *wise + wella → Wisewell 1207). Early forms, such as Wiswall 1491, frequently have '-a-' instead of '-e-' in the second element, probably showing Mercian influence.

Withington *tūn* among willow-trees (OE *wiðign + tūn → Wythinton 1212 → Wythington 1246). The site is low-lying. Compare *WINTON*.

Withnell hill where willows grow (OE *wiðign + hyll → Withinhull c.1160 → Wenehull C.1250 → Withnell 1557). The name appears in the hamlets of WITHNELL FOLD (OE fald, 'fold, enclosure for animals') and WITHNELL MILL. The present WITHNELL MOOR was formerly 'Gunnolf's or Gunnell's moors' (ON Gunnulf(r) + -es (possessive) + mōr → Gunnoluesmores 1212 → Gunnolemores post-1250).

Witton ? *tūn* in a wood (OE wudu/widu + tūn → Witton 1246). The name refers to a large area of parkland west of Blackburn, from the R Darwen to Billinge Hill. The usual OE form of the proposed first element is wudu; widu is an earlier form of the word which generally disappears from the eighth century but is found in a few place-names. OE Witta, a personal name, has also been proposed for the first element.

Wolfhole Crag ? the wolf's lair (OE wulf + halh → Woffal 1284 → Wolfalle 1285 → Wolfalcrag c.1350). The second element presents some difficulty. OE halh would here have the sense of 'hollow in a hillside'; but OE hol, 'hole', would also be possible and has certainly been influential in the name's development. Yet another possibility is ON fjall, 'fell', which, referring to a single mountain, would give good sense for a height of 1,731 feet. Whatever the etymology, the phrase had become a name when CRAG (ME cragge, 'crag, rock') was added. The reduction of the second element is well illustrated in forms such as Wulfo Crag 1577 and Wulfcragge 1577.

Wolfstones A minor name referring to a boundary mark near Colne, at 1,455 feet. The name may be self-explanatory, or the first element could be the OE personal name Wulfa.

Woodbroughton See *BROUGHTON*.

Woodhouses enclosure in the wood (OE wudu + haga → Woodheyes pre-1390). The name refers to an enclosure for which permission was granted to John de Assheton in 1377). The second element has later been replaced by HOUSES.

Woodland land covered with wood (OE wudu + land → Kirkeby wodelands 1544 → Wodland 1577). The hamlet is near Kirkby Ireleth, to

151

which the wood evidently belonged.

Woodplumpton the *PLUMPTON* in the wood (OE wudu + PLUMPTON → Plunton DB → Plumpton 1256 → Wodeplumpton 1327). The name was originally PLUMPTON, 'plum-tree *tūn'*, to which WOOD has been added to distinguish the place from FIELD PLUMPTON. See *PLUMPTON*.

Woolston Wulf's *tūn* (OE Wulf + -es (possessive) + tūn → Wolueston 1246 → Wolston 1327). It has been suggested that the first element is a compound-name, such as OE Wulfsige, which has been shortened. Influence from ON ulfr, 'wolf', is seen in Ulfitonam 1142 (Latin). The earliest recorded form of the name is Oscitonam 1094 (Latin), but this is generally disregarded as an error.

Woolton Wulfa's *tūn* (OE Wulfa + tūn). Records distinguish MUCH and LITTLE WOOLTON on occasion (Vlventune DB → Wolueton c.1180 → Wlueton 1187 → Parua Wolton c.1190/Magna Wlueton c.1250). The records show a variety of different forms. Forms with initial Ulv-/Wlv-, such as the DB form or those of 1187 and c.1250, show influence from ON ulfr, 'wolf'; the frequency of such forms suggests a large Scandinavian element in the population of the area and may even indicate a Scandinavian owner of the *tūn*, although the *tūn*-form and also the development of the first element are characteristically English. A number of forms, including that in DB above – to which may be added Wlvinton 1188 and Wolventon 1323 – show the '-n-' of the possessive inflection, OE Wulfan,

which distinguishes this name from the '-s-' form in *WOOLSTON*.

Worsaw etymology doubtful (Worsow 1529). The second element is presumably OE hōh, 'spur of rock', or ON haugr, 'hill', appropriate to a 725-foot limestone knoll, but there is no obvious source for the first element and forms are late.

Worsley ? Weorcgyth's *lēah* (OE *Weorcgȳð + -es (possessive) + lēah → Werkesleia 1196 (Latin) → Wyrkedele 1212 → Wirkithileg 1246 → Wurkythesle 1246 → Workesleye 1300). The first element is probably a personal name, but forms suggest two different bases – one compounded (e.g. the 1246 forms) and the other shortened to *Weorc-es (e.g. the earliest form); no such personal name has, however, been recorded. A number of forms (e.g. that of 1212) lack the possessive -es inflection. The name also appears in WORSLEY MESNE (WORSLEY + Fr. mesne, 'demesne').

Worsthorne Worth's thorn-bush (OE Weorð + -es (possessive) + þorn → Wrthesthorn c.1200 → Worthesthorn 1202). The name probably refers to a thorn-bush which served as a boundary-mark for Worth's lands. Derivation from OE worð, 'enclosure', is unlikely. See *HURSTWOOD*.

Worston Worth's *tūn* (OE Weorð + -es (possessive) + tūn → Wrtheston 1242 → Wurtheston 1285 → Worstcn 1311).

Worthington *tūn* associated with Worth (OE Weorð + -*ingtūn* → Wrthinton c.1225 → Worthinton 1243 → Wurthington 1246). The name may be of the *-ingatūn* type, perhaps indicative of early Anglo-Saxon settlement (see introduction p. 46). Other etymologies proposed for the first element include OE worðign, 'enclosure', and a personal name with possessive inflection, OE *Worpan, neither of which seems probable.

Wrampool the crooked stream (ON (v)rangr/OE wrang + OE pōl/OE *pull → Wrangepul 1230). The name refers to a nearby stream.

Wray corner of land (ON vrá). The name of two places:
(1) near *BOTTON* (Wra c.1200); the name refers to an eight mile strip of fell along the R. Hindburn, and the village is at the foot of the valley in the north, where the R. Roeburn joins the Hindburn;
(2) near Claife (Wraye c.1535), divided into HIGH WRAY (Heywray 1619) and LOW WRAY, in a steep and wooded area.

Wrayton *tūn* in a corner of land (ON vrá + OE tūn → Wraton 1210 → Wraiton 1229). The village is on the R. Greeta, but off the main valley. See *MELLING*.

Wrea Green corner of land (ON vrá → Wra 1201). GREEN is a later addition — the village green is the largest surviving in Lancashire. See *RIBBY*.

Wrightington ? *tūn* of the wrights, i.e. of those who work in wood (OE wyrht + -ena (possessive pl.) + tūn → Wrichtington 1202).

Wrynose Pass stallion's ridge (ON vreini + hals → Wreineshals c.1160 → Wrenhalse c.1160 → Wrenosse Hill 1577). The name has been re-formed in a more familiar pattern by popular etymology. The pass is the watershed between the rivers Duddon and Brathay.

Wycoller *wīc* among alder trees (OE wīc + alor → Wycoluer 1324).

Wymott Brook (R) etymology doubtful(Wimoth c.1215 → Wymote 1547). It has been suggested that the second element is OE mūða, 'mouth', referring to the junction of the brook with the R. Lostock, and that the first element is a Celtic river-name. Compare *WYRE*.

Wyre (R) winding river (Celt. *vigorā → Wir 1184). The name would describe the meandering course of the river across the flat plain of the Fylde.

Wyresdale valley of the R. *WYRE* (WYRE + ON dalr), seen in NETHER WYRESDALE (Wiresdale 1190 → Nether Weiresdale 1517) and OVER WYRESDALE (Wyrsedale 1246).

Y

Yarrow (R) rough river (cf. Celt. *garwo- → Yarwe c.1190 → Yarewe 1246). The name would most appropriately describe the upper reaches of the river.

Yarlside the hill pasture belonging to a nobleman (OB jarl + sætr → Yerleshed Cott 1509 → Yerlyssyde Cote c.1525).

Yate Bank gap in the hills (OE geat → Yatebank 1588). The reference is to a small valley between spurs of high moorland rising to over 1,000 feet. BANK, from ON banke, 'slope of a hill', has been added later.

Yealand high land (OE hēah + land → Jalant DB → Yeland 1190 → Hielande 1202). The manor was divided after the Norman Conquest into:
(1) YEALAND CONYERS (Yelannd Coygners 1301), held by Robert de Conyers in 1242 – the family name is a French place-name;
(2) YEALAND REDMAYNE (Yeland Redman 1395), held by the Redman or Redmayne family in the twelfth century – the family-name is a Cumberland place-name.
The name also occurs in
(3) YEALAND STORRS (YEALAND + ON storð, 'wood' → Yelondstorthes 1558 → Yealand Stors 1593), 'wood belonging to YEALAND'. The final element recurs in nearby *STORRS MOSS*, evidently referring to the same feature.
The name is difficult to interpret and OE ēa, 'stream', referring to the Leighton Beck near Yealand Conyers, has also been suggested as the first element.

Yewdale yew-tree valley (OE īw + ON dalr → Ywedalebec 1196).